Good News on the Frontier

a history of the Cumberland Presbyterian Church

Thomas H. Campbell

The Covenant Life Curriculum

PUBLISHED BY

frontier press

MEMPHIS, TENNESSEE

THE COVENANT LIFE CURRICULUM

the authorized curriculum
of the following denominations

Associate Reformed Presbyterian Church

Cumberland Presbyterian Church

Moravian Church in America

Presbyterian Church in the United States

Reformed Church in America

285.13509
C 153

160777

© Frontier Press 1965

Contents

Preface

THIS SERIES OF studies was originally undertaken to provide a resource book for use in youth conferences, leadership education schools and classes, and other settings. The suggestion was made that it be arranged in thirteen chapters so that it might also be used as an elective course of study by youth and adult classes in the Sunday school. When the Covenant Life Curriculum was adopted as the curriculum of the Cumberland Presbyterian Church, it was planned that the second year of a three-year cycle would be a study of church history. Dr. Ernest Trice Thompson's book, *Through the Ages,* will be used by all the participating denominations for nine months, and each denomination will devote three months to the study of its own history. This book is intended to serve as the textbook for Cumberland Presbyterians in the study of their history.

Some twenty years ago the author wrote a book entitled *Studies in Cumberland Presbyterian History,* which also was designed as a textbook for use in the Leadership Education Curriculum of the Cumberland Presbyterian Church. This book is now out of print. Much of the material and some of the phraseology found in the earlier book may be recognized in the present series of studies; however, this effort represents a complete rewriting rather than a revision of the former work. The author's more recent study has led him to believe that although Cumberland Presbyterians should not be unmindful of their rich heritage from the Presbyterian and Reformed tradition there are other aspects of their heritage without a knowledge of which the distinctive character of the Cumberland Presbyterian Church cannot be understood. Therefore attention has been given to the influences deriving from the Arminian and pietist traditions. It was felt, too, that more attention should be given the relation of the

Cumberland Presbyterian Church to its Negro constituency, both before and during the period of the separate existence of a Negro Cumberland Presbyterian Church, than was given in the earlier treatment. Also, three whole chapters have been given to the development and progress of the Cumberland Presbyterian Church since the attempted union with the Presbyterian Church, U. S. A., which was formally consummated in 1906.

Unfortunately no full scale history of the Cumberland Presbyterian Church has appeared since Dr. B. W. McDonnold's monumental *History of the Cumberland Presbyterian Church,* which was first published in 1888, and this work has been out of print for many years. Consequently there is a dearth of available historical material concerning the Cumberland Presbyterian Church available to the average reader. This lack could not be remedied in the present series of studies, for due to limitations of space it was necessary to select those aspects of Cumberland Presbyterian history which it appeared would best convey to the reader the distinctive character of the Cumberland Presbyterian Church as revealed by its history. It is gratifying to know that an effort is being made to remedy this deficiency, however. A new definitive history of the Cumberland Presbyterian Church, in which four historians are co-operating, is now in process of preparation for publication at an early date, perhaps sometime during 1966.

Since it was necessary to be selective in regard to the material to be condensed within the necessary limits of this series of studies, it seemed fitting to organize this series around the understanding of the Cumberland Presbyterian Church as a church of the frontier. The Cumberland Presbyterian Church had its origin on the frontier and as a result of conditions on the frontier and has derived much of its character from this fact. Its founders and those who labored with them kept abreast of the advancing frontier, bringing the "good news" of Christ to the people who were on the growing edge of the new nation. The Cumberland Presbyterian Church has been at its best when it has remembered its true character as a church of the frontier.

It is hoped that through this series of studies Cumberland Presbyterians may achieve a clearer understanding of the origin and progress of that branch of God's visible church through which they are serving and that through the story of the Cumberland Presbyterian Church they may be inspired to face with courage and faith the new frontiers which challenge those who have a part in proclaiming the "good news" of the kingdom of God today.

THOMAS H. CAMPBELL

Memphis, Tennessee

March 3, 1965

1. Our American Denominational Pattern

IN THIS STUDY we shall be concerned with a particular denomination of the Christian church. It is a denomination which had its origin on the North American continent. Although the multiplicity of denominations to which we are accustomed is largely an American phenomenon, the diversity in Christian beliefs and practices which gave rise to the existence of denominations had its roots in Europe.

If there ever was a time when all Christians held identical interpretations of the gospel or were absolutely uniform in their practices, that time was of short duration. A variety of beliefs and practices began to develop as early as the New Testament period. However, with the development of a strong central church government (first under the leadership of the bishop of a local church or area, and later under the bishop of Rome who gradually gained ascendancy over his fellow bishops), leaders of the church were able to establish a norm of doctrines and practices, to require adherence to that norm, and to discourage deviation from the established norm. Those who persisted in the preaching of "heresy" were excommunicated from the church and often sent into exile.

HOW DENOMINATIONS BEGAN

Although the separation of eastern (Orthodox) and western

(Roman Catholic) churches occurred in 1054, the Roman Catholic Church continued to dominate the West and to maintain at least an outward show of unity until the time of the Reformation. The Roman Catholic Church taught that the church, rather than the Scriptures, was the final authority on questions of faith and conduct; that the individual was not competent to interpret the Scriptures for himself but must look to the church to interpret them for him; and that none could be saved except through the sacraments of the church administered by priests who derived their authority from bishops who were supposed to stand in a direct succession from the apostles—especially from St. Peter to whom had been given the keys of the kingdom.

Later, during the medieval period (which extended from *ca.* 500 A.D.-1450 A.D.), more stringent measures were used to suppress individuals and groups of Christians who refused to conform to the established beliefs and practices of the Roman Catholic Church. John Huss, a Bohemian Christian who was a forerunner of the Protestant Reformation, was burned at the stake. Attempts were made to exterminate groups such as the Waldensians and Albigensians who dared preach against what they regarded as corrupt practices of the Roman Catholic Church.

The Protestant Reformation began in 1516 under the leadership of Martin Luther. Luther advocated three main principles which resulted in his exclusion from the Roman Catholic Church: (1) the doctrine of justification by faith, which means that man is saved by faith alone, and not through good works; (2) the doctrine of an "open Bible," which means that each person should be permitted to read the Bible for himself and that the Scriptures, rather than the decisions of church councils, are the only infallible rule of faith and practice; and (3) the doctrine of the priesthood of believers, which means that all Christians stand in the relation of priests in that each can approach God through Christ and each stands in a relation of being a priest in behalf of his brethren.

Acceptance of the first and third principles meant doing away with the necessity of a mediatorial priesthood as interpreted by those who called themselves "Catholic." Acceptance of the second meant shifting the seat of authority from the church to the

Scriptures and opened the way for holding diverse opinions as to the teachings of Scripture.

Differing interpretations of Scripture opened the way for divisions based upon these differences. Such differences might not have been so divisive in their effects if a spirit of tolerance had always prevailed. As Dr. George P. Fisher points out, the divisions within Protestantism "arose generally from the spirit of intolerance, and the spirit of faction; two tempers of feeling which have an identical root, since both grow out of a disposition to push to an extreme, even to the point of exclusion and separation, religious opinions which may be the property of an individual or of a class, but are not fundamental to the Christian faith." [1] As an illustration of this spirit the instance may be cited of Martin Luther's refusing to regard Ulrich Zwingli and his Swiss companions as Christian brethren, and even refusing to accept the right hand of fellowship proffered him by Zwingli, because there was not complete agreement between them regarding the Lord's Supper. Luther did a great work for the cause of Christian liberty, but he seemed to think that Christians must agree on all points of doctrine in order to have fellowship with one another.

Divisions began to occur among Protestants at an early stage in the history of the Reformation. The first of these was the result of the Eucharistic controversy. Luther and Zwingli began their work about the same time, Luther in Germany and Zwingli in Switzerland. On most points—such as the supreme authority of the Scriptures, justification by faith, and the rejection of the claims of the papacy—they were in agreement. They disagreed, however, on the meaning of the words of Jesus in the institution of the Lord's Supper. Both contended that the cup, as well as the bread, should be served to the people. Both rejected the doctrine of transubstantiation—the teaching of the Roman Catholic Church that the bread and wine used in the Eucharist actually become the body and blood of Christ. But Luther believed that in some mysterious way the body and blood of Christ are present and are received by the communicant; that although the bread and wine are not changed, Christ's glorified body is somehow present in them, so that there are really two substances present. Hence, the name consubstantiation has been given to Luther's doctrine. Zwingli, on the other hand, regarded the Lord's Supper simply as a service in which the death of Christ is commemorated, and as a token that Christ is present to the contemplative faith of the believer.

In an attempt to unite the two parties, a conference was arranged which Luther and Zwingli both attended. But Luther refused to be moved from his position, and, while those present were seated around the table, he wrote with a piece of chalk, *"hoc est meum corpus"* ("this is my body"), thus expressing his refusal to think of the words of Christ in any other than a literal sense. Zwingli cited such passages as "I am the true vine," which are generally accepted as having only a figurative meaning.

John Calvin, who came on the scene after the death of Zwingli but during the lifetime of Luther, took a "middle ground" between the two views. In doing so he incurred the displeasure of the Lutherans while he succeeded in attaining union with the Zwinglian churches. Calvin affirmed the *spiritual* presence of Christ in the Lord's Supper and taught that the benefits of Christ's presence are received only by the believer. Thus occurred the division which resulted in the formation of the Lutheran churches on the one hand and the Reformed (Presbyterian) churches on the other. Among the followers of Calvin was John Knox, who led in the opposition to Roman Catholicism in Scotland and the establishment of the Presbyterian Church there.

In the meantime the Church of England had broken its ties with Rome. Henry VIII was king and certainly was no Protestant. In fact, he had written a discourse against Luther which caused the Pope to confer on him the title "Defender of the Faith," a title which the sovereigns of England have since worn. His controversy with the Pope developed when he attempted to have his marriage with Catherine of Aragon annulled in order that he might marry Anne Boleyn. It was not uncommon in that period of history for the Pope to annul a marriage if it suited his purpose to do so, but at this particular time he was involved in war in which he needed the help of Catherine's brother, King Philip of

Spain. He refused to grant the annulment, whereupon Henry VIII severed the relation of the church in England with Rome and made himself head of the Church of England.

In this action the king had the support of a group of Protestants in England. After Henry's death the Church of England became Protestant under Edward VI but reverted to Roman Catholicism for a short time during the reign of Mary I. The next queen, Elizabeth I, embraced Protestantism but demanded uniformity of faith and worship on the part of her subjects. During her reign the Thirty-Nine Articles, which since have constituted the doctrinal standard of the Church of England, were written. The prayer book retained much of the ancient liturgy but it was put into the English language. Although there has been much discussion as to whether the Church of England is Catholic or Protestant, the Thirty-Nine Articles generally reflect a Protestant viewpoint. Thus came into existence a third major branch of Protestantism.

The purpose of the Reformers, as the word indicates, was to "reform" the existing church. Neither Luther nor any of the other Reformers had any intention, at first, of founding a new church or of breaking with the Roman Catholic Church. They were seeking to correct the erroneous practices which they saw going on within the church. Even after they were excommunicated from the Roman Church, they sought to utilize the existing political institutions and to make them what they ought to be rather than destroy them. There were some people, however, who thought the Reformers had not gone far enough. They advocated more revolutionary changes. One such group was the various sects known as Anabaptists.

The Anabaptists took their name from the fact that they required persons joining them to be baptized again even though these persons had been baptized in infancy. They rejected infant baptism. All Anabaptists did not believe and practice the same things. Some contended that only the saints should rule, so they attempted to seize the reins of government as revolutionists. Others taught that, because the existing political institutions were evil, Christians should stay aloof from them altogether. Therefore, they refused to hold office, take oaths, or serve in the army. The most important of the latter class were the Mennonites, who derived their name from their leader, Menno Simons.

There were others who took the position of refusing to accept that which seemed to them to be contrary to reason. Consequently, as they could not understand the doctrine of the Trinity, they rejected it. They taught that Jesus was not divine but was simply a great teacher and lawgiver. Because their principal leader was Socinus, those holding this form of doctrine are sometimes called Socinians.

DENOMINATIONS TRANSPLANTED TO AMERICA

The people who came to America were from many different countries and backgrounds and brought their religious teachings with them. Those who settled at Jamestown, Virginia, in 1607 were members of the Church of England. This church became the established church (that is, the church supported by the government) in Virginia, the Carolinas, Georgia, and, for a period of time, in Maryland. The Pilgrims who landed at Plymouth in 1620 were Puritans who had separated from the Church of England. The Puritans who came a few years later to Massachusetts Bay, Connecticut, and New Haven still considered themselves members of the Church of England, but they soon set up their own churches under a congregational form of government. They, together with the Plymouth colonists, became known in America as Congregationalists. Although they had come to America in search of religious freedom, they were not always willing to grant it to those who differed with them. Thus Roger Williams was driven out of Massachusetts and found refuge in Rhode Island where he established at Providence the first Baptist church in America.

To the middle colonies came people representing a variety of religious groups. Roman Catholics led in the settlement of Maryland which was the first colony established in America in which all religious groups were to have freedom to worship God as they chose. New York (first called New Amsterdam) was settled by the Dutch, and the Dutch Reformed Church was the predominant church there. Pennsylvania, although established on the basis of providing religious freedom for all, was colonized by a Quaker and became a haven for members of this group who were facing persecution in England or in the other colonies. To the middle colonies came also such groups as the Mennonites, the Dunkers (German Baptists), the Schwenkfelders, German Lutherans, and Moravians. A group of German Lutherans known as the Salzburgers settled in Georgia and South Carolina, thus introducing Lutheranism to that area.

Presbyterians in considerable numbers also migrated to America, a few from England, some from Scotland, but larger numbers from north Ireland. Following the subjugation of the native Irish chieftains by the English, the confiscated estates in northern Ireland had been made available for colonization during the reign of James I under whom the kingdoms of England and Scotland were united. Most of the colonists who came to Ireland were from Scotland, hence the name Scotch-Irish which came to be applied to them. They were, of course, Presbyterians. Beginning in about the year 1686 and continuing well into the eighteenth century the Scotch-Irish migrated in large numbers to the American colonies. The first presbytery in America was organized under the leadership of Francis Makemie in Philadelphia in 1706. Groups of Scotch dissenters who had separated from the established Church of Scotland also came to America, and through their efforts both Associate and Reformed presbyteries were organized in the New World.

Altogether representatives of at least fifteen different "denominations" migrated to America prior to the War for Independence. This does not include the Methodists who still were officially members of the Church of England.

NEW DENOMINATIONS SINCE INDEPENDENCE

With the achievement of independence the churches in America soon began setting up their own national organizations. John Wesley advised the Methodist societies in America to form a separate organization apart from the Church of England and ordained Thomas Coke and Francis Asbury as superintendents to effect this organization. Soon afterward, bishops were brought over to constitute the Protestant Episcopal Church out of the constituents of the Church of England in this country.

In 1785 the state of Virginia passed a measure granting religious freedom within the state. The national Constitution written in 1787 prohibited the establishment of any church by Congress. Whatever remaining establishments still existed in the older states were soon to disappear. This made it possible for churches to divide and subdivide at will, and the way was open for a further multiplication of denominations.

William Warren Sweet lists the following as the main causes for division among the churches in America since the achievement of independence: (1) revivals, (2) slavery and secession, (3) doctrine, (4) church rites and practices, and (5) church government.[2]

Out of the Revival of 1800 in Kentucky came the Cumberland Presbyterians and the "Christians." A portion of the latter group, under the leadership of Barton W. Stone, joined forces with Alexander Campbell to form the Disciples of Christ. The remainder united with the Republican Methodists to form the "Christian Connection" which in turn united with the Congregational churches in 1929. The story of the Cumberland Presbyterians is the concern of the present study.

The slavery controversy brought into existence the Methodist Episcopal Church, South, and the Southern Baptist Convention. Measures taken in the General Assembly of the Presbyterian Church, U. S. A., Old School, in 1861 to condemn the secession of the southern states resulted in the creation of the Presbyterian Church in the Confederate States of America, now known as the Presbyterian Church, U. S.

A controversy over church government resulted in the formation of the Methodist Protestant Church in 1830. The Methodist Protestants had contended without avail for lay representation in the conferences. Methodist conferences at that time were made up solely of ministers.

An example of a division involving worship practices is the

division among the Disciples of Christ which resulted in the formation about the year 1900 of the Churches of Christ. The latter group opposed the use of instrumental music in church worship.

Doctrinal issues brought into existence the various holiness groups which sprang up in the latter part of the nineteenth century. These groups emphasized the doctrine of sanctification as a second distinct work of grace after regeneration.

Mention should also be made of groups which migrated to the United States after 1800. Prominent among these were the Lutherans who formed the Missouri Synod, Swedish Lutherans who formed the Augustana Synod, Norwegian Lutherans, Greek Orthodox, and others. Each of these groups perpetuated its own congregations in its new home.

GAINS AND LOSSES

The multiplication of denominations within Protestantism has been a target of criticism both from within and from without the Protestant churches. The critical comments most frequently heard are (1) that competition and intolerance as displayed by the various denominations toward one another impede the progress of Christianity by giving the wrong impression to an unbelieving world; (2) that needless duplication of effort often results, since a number of small churches are often found within a single community; and (3) that Protestant Christianity cannot present the united front against the forces of evil which otherwise would be possible.

Too often divisions have occurred as a result of differences over trivial matters, a desire for the promotion of personal ambition, or an unwillingness to seek earnestly to resolve existing differences. A broader toleration of differences in belief and practice and a willingness to recognize and utilize the peculiar gifts of those who did not conform to the norm might have prevented many of the divisions which have occurred.

On the other hand, as Dr. Fisher has pointed out,

"On this subject of denominational or sectarian divisions it may be said with truth, that division of this sort is better than a leaden uniformity, the effect of blind obedience to ecclesiastical superiors, of the stagnation of religious thought, or of coercion. Disagreement in opinion is a penalty of intellectual activity, to which it is well to submit where the alternative is either of the evils just mentioned." [3]

Another church historian has said,

"It would be a very unwise policy, even if it were possible to do away with denominations. All people do not care to worship alike, and all people cannot work under the same organization. We need variety in the Church, we need all types and classes in the Church, and we need many organized bodies working for one common end—the kingdom of God." [4]

As long as people read the Bible for themselves, there are going to be differences of interpretation. Other factors, such as social issues, have also entered into the picture. No one denomination has a monopoly on the truth and each may contribute some element of truth or some emphasis that was not given adequate expression in the denominations already existing. Therefore, we should think of our various denominations, not as in competition with one another, but as co-operating with one another and complementing one another, each contributing of the gifts which the Spirit of God has bestowed upon it.

SOMETHING TO THINK ABOUT

1. What denominations are represented in your community? What do you know concerning their origin and history?

2. Is it possible to maintain the ideal of an "open Bible" (the right of all Christians to read the Bible for themselves) and at the same time maintain uniformity in beliefs and church practices?

3. To what extent should uniformity of belief be enforced as a condition of belonging to a particular denomination?

4. Although some of the American colonies once had established churches (churches supported by the government), these establishments have long since disappeared. What circumstances made it impossible or impractical to maintain them?

5. Some of the causes for division of churches on the American scene have been noted. Why has it been difficult to reunite churches which have become divided even though the issues which divided them (e.g., slavery and secession) have long since ceased to be issues?

6. List some particular contributions the various denominations have made to the religious life of people without which the community would have been spiritually poorer.

7. In what ways has the Cumberland Presbyterian Church contributed to the spiritual life of people whom you know? What contributions has it made to your own life as a Christian?

2. What Cumberland Presbyterians Inherited

CUMBERLAND PRESBYTERIANS SHARE in a heritage which dates back to New Testament times and earlier. In a sense it is true that the things which unite Cumberland Presbyterians with other evangelical Christians are more important and more numerous than those which separate the various branches of the church universal from one another. Yet a proper understanding of history requires that attention be given to some of the more important strands of heritage which have given to the Cumberland Presbyterian Church its distinctive characteristics.

FROM THE PRESBYTERIAN AND
REFORMED TRADITION

The word "Presbyterian" has reference to church government rather than to doctrine. To be Presbyterian implies a government by "presbyters" or "elders." Presbyterians generally have believed that this was the form of government used in the congregation of Israel in Old Testament times and that, after the ascension of Christ, this same type of government was perpetuated in the Christian churches. Presbyterians hold that the Greek words translated "elder" and "bishop" originally referred to the same office, and that the exaltation of one elder in a church to the office of bishop was a later development. An example of the synonymous use of the two terms is found in the account of Paul's address to the elders of the church at Ephesus (Acts 20:17ff.). While the historian speaks of them as "elders" (verse 17), Paul speaks of "the flock, in which the Holy Spirit hath made you bishops" (verse 28, American Standard Version).

Presbyterians recognize two kinds of elders, teaching elders and ruling elders. These differ, not in office, but in function. Thus in 1 Timothy 5:17 the writer says, "Let the elders that rule well be counted worthy of double honor, especially they who labor in the word and doctrine."

The office of deacon, it is believed, was created in the church during the apostolic period to take care of the temporal affairs of the church, thus freeing the elders to devote themselves to "prayer" and "the ministry of the word" (Acts 6:1-4).

Presbyterian government differs from congregational government in that, while it recognizes that local churches originally were, and ought to be, governed by their elders, it also recognizes the right of representative councils or synods to rule in matters which concern a number of churches. Thus the Council at Jerusalem ruled upon the question as to whether Gentiles should be admitted into the churches without first becoming Jews (Acts 15:1-31).

Neither Luther nor Zwingli paid much attention to the question of church government. It remained for John Calvin to organize the Reformed churches along presbyterian lines.

Calvin was born at Noyon, France, July 10, 1509, and was converted to Protestantism in about the year 1533. In 1536 he came to the city of Geneva intending only to spend the night. William Farel, who was already preaching the Protestant doctrines in Geneva, heard of his being there and urged him to stay and assist in the work. He was finally persuaded to remain after Farel had invoked a curse upon him if he persisted in his refusal.

In Geneva, John Calvin organized the first Presbyterian church of the Reformation. In it there were four orders of church officers: pastors, doctors (meaning teachers of theology in the school which was to be set up for the training of ministers), elders, and deacons. He was unable entirely to disengage the church government from the civil government, as the latter had some authority in the election of church officers; but he fought, and finally won, a battle to secure to the church the exclusive right to say who should be allowed to commune at the Lord's table. Many of the disciplinary measures put into effect under Calvin's influence were severe, acording to our way of thinking, but a great change for the better was effected in the character and reputation of the city. Geneva was too small a territory to set up a synod or a General Assembly, but Calvin held to this phase of presbyterian government in theory and assisted in writing the constitution by which the synod of the French Protestants, or Huguenots, was governed. This also became the form of government of the Reformed churches in Holland.

Calvin was also a theologian. At the age of twenty-six, he had already written the first edition of the *Institutes of the Christian Religion,* which was to become the textbook of presbyterianism. He taught that by the fall of man the image of God in him was so corrupted that man has neither the power nor the will to do good. God, however, in order to demonstrate his mercy, chose to rescue a certain portion of the human race from its lost estate. Christ died for these "elect" persons; they are called of God by an irresistible call, and faith is given them so that they lay hold upon salvation. The non-elect, on the other hand, are left to suffer the just punishment for their sins. Although Luther, too, believed in unconditional election, it was Calvin who made this doctrine the foundation stone in his system.

Geneva became a haven for persecuted groups in Scotland and England. John Knox, who later became the leader in the reformation of the church in Scotland, received his instruction here. So did the English refugees from the "blood bath" of Queen Mary's reign. These later returned to England to become the leaders in the Puritan movement there.

The Presbyterian Church became, under the leadership of John Knox, the established church of Scotland. The Puritans who returned to England were unable to make much headway toward getting their ideas accepted. The church there remained episcopal in government throughout the reigns of Elizabeth I and James I. The Puritans gained the ascendancy, however, during the reign of Charles I and started a revolution which overthrew both the monarchy and the episcopacy. In 1643, the English Parliament called an assembly of ministers and laymen to give advice with reference to the doctrine, government, and liturgy of the Church of England. This assembly is known in history as the Westminster Assembly, and the Confession of Faith it formulated is known as the Westminster Confession. In this assembly the Scotch commissioners exerted great influence so that it was decided to organize the Church of England along presbyterian lines. The doctrines of John Calvin were adopted. A Directory for Worship giving only general instructions about the services was designed to replace the prayer book.

The Church of England never became Presbyterian, however, for two reasons. First, the English people knew little or nothing about Presbyterian government, and, second, Oliver Cromwell, who came to power about that time, was not a Presbyterian but an Independent (Congregationalist). Although the Westminster Confession was little used in England, it became the standard of the Presbyterian churches in Scotland, Ireland, and America.

The majority of the Presbyterians who migrated to America were Scotch-Irish; that is to say, Scotch who had settled in northern Ireland. Here they were soon subjected to persecution, for the Church of England was the established church here, and the Presbyterian Church could number among its members only those who adhered to it voluntarily. This condition, however, produced a hardiness of character and a love of liberty which were imparted to the church in America.

The first presbytery in America was organized at Philadelphia in 1706. In 1716 this presbytery was divided into four presbyteries, and a synod was organized. In 1729 this synod passed the Adopting Act, which required all ministers coming into any of the presbyteries to subscribe to the Westminster Confession.

When Cumberland Presbytery was organized in 1810, its members did not accept all the teachings of the church out of which they came, yet their Presbyterian heritage is apparent in several particulars:

(1) The Presbyterian form of government was adopted, al-

though with some modifications to meet the needs of the frontier.

(2) The Westminster Confession of Faith was adopted by the reorganized Cumberland Presbytery in 1810 as its Confession "except the idea of fatality, that seems to be taught under the mysterious doctrine of predestination." Provision was made, however, for the ordination of those who could accept the Westminster Confession without exception.

(3) Cumberland Presbyterians inherited the Presbyterian emphasis on Christian character as the outcome of salvation.

(4) Cumberland Presbyterians inherited an appreciation for an educated ministry, although in practice they made adaptations to meet the needs of the frontier.

(5) Cumberland Presbyterians accepted, although not without a struggle, the Presbyterian system of settled pastorates.

(6) Cumberland Presbyterians inherited the Presbyterian nonliturgical worship as set forth in the Directory for Worship already mentioned.

FROM ARMINIANISM

Jacob Arminius was born at Oudewater, Holland, in 1560, and died in Leyden in 1609. In 1575, the University of Leyden was founded by William the Silent, liberator of the Dutch people from the Roman Catholic yoke, and Arminius was enrolled there as a student. At the age of twenty-one he was sent to the University of Geneva where he attended the lectures of Theodore Beza, successor to Calvin. In 1589, while serving as pastor of a Reformed church in Amsterdam, Arminius was invited to reply to a critic of ultra-Calvinism, one Theodore Koornhert. As he prepared himself for a discussion of the subject, he became convinced of the unethical character of an arbitrary decree by which certain individuals were supposed to be foreordained to damnation. Going back to the Bible and the church fathers, he attacked the view of unconditional predestination which had grown up within the Calvinist tradition.

Arminius was concerned to establish two things: (1) That God is not the author of sin, as Calvinism seemed to imply, and

(2) that man is responsible for his sins. Arminius contended that man cannot be held responsible for that which he cannot help doing. If man is predestined in his total life, Arminius reasoned, sin is impossible and the condemnation of sin unethical. Unconditional predestination, far from glorifying God, was seen as actually dethroning him, for if this doctrine be true, Arminius said, "God is the only sinner." [1] It also dishonors Christ, for salvation depends not upon Christ and his work but upon a prior decree of election. The nerve of evangelism is cut, for those who believe themselves to be among the "elect" suffer from unethical complacency, while those who believe themselves predestined to damnation suffer from unnecessary despair.[2]

On the positive side, Arminius taught what may be termed conditional predestination. God decreed the appointment of his Son, Jesus Christ, as Mediator, Redeemer, and Savior. He also decreed the salvation of *"those who repent and believe,"* and left in sin *"all impenitent persons and unbelievers."* [3] On the basis of his foreknowledge of men's responses, God did indeed decree the salvation and damnation of particular persons, but this was different from the Calvinistic position that God decreed the salvation and damnation of certain persons apart from any foreknowledge of faith or good works.

Arminius by no means minimized the importance or necessity of the grace of God, but he defined grace as proffered goodness, not an irresistible force. The fact that man possesses freedom of will to respond or refuse to respond does not make salvation any less of grace. "A rich man bestows on a poor and famishing beggar, alms by which he may be able to maintain himself and his family. Does it cease to be a pure gift (grace) because the beggar extends his hand to receive it (free will)?" [4]

In 1610 (the year after Arminius died), his followers published the Five Articles of the Remonstrants. In substance these were (1) that God determined before the foundation of the world to save believers and condemn the unbelieving; (2) that Christ died for all men; (3) that it is necessary for man to be born again before he can understand, think, will, and perform what is truly good; (4) that the grace of God is necessary for man to think, will, or do any good thing, but that this grace is not irresistible; and (5) that the believer is given adequate power to strive against sin, but that the question whether the believer may through sloth or negligence forsake his life in Christ must be the subject of more exact inquiry in the Holy Scriptures.

In 1618, the Synod of Dort condemned the doctrines of Arminius as set forth in the Articles of the Remonstrants and reasserted the so-called five points of Calvinism: (1) total depravity, (2) unconditional election, (3) prevenient and irresistible grace, (4) perseverance of the saints, and (5) limited atonement. Arminian pastors were banished from Holland. Yet Arminianism lived on within the Anglican Church and was revived by John Wesley in the eighteenth century.

Cumberland Presbyterians have often referred to their system of doctrine as a "middle ground" between Calvinism and Arminianism. In this writer's opinion, a comparison of the Cumberland Presbyterian Confession of Faith with the Articles of the Remonstrants, however, suggests that Cumberland Presbyterians are more Arminian than Calvinist. Cumberland Presbyterians are in substantial agreement with all the Articles of the Remonstrants except the one which questions the perseverance of the saints. On the other hand, the perseverance of the saints is the only one of the five points of Calvinism, as set forth by the Synod of Dort, that Cumberland Presbyterians accept, and they do not accept it in its Calvinistic form. In the Westminster Confession the perseverence of the saints is based upon, among other things, "the unchangeable decree of election." The *elect* cannot fall away and be lost, for God has decreed otherwise. Cumberland Presbyterians, on the other hand, do not say that the truly regenerated man *cannot* fall, but that he *will not* fall. This conviction they base not on an unchangeable decree of election but upon "the unchangeable love and power of God, the merits, advocacy, and intercession of Jesus Christ, the abiding of the Holy Spirit and seed of God within them, and the nature of the Covenant of Grace."

The doctrinal position Cumberland Presbyterians came to hold was, like the position taken by Arminius, a protest against certain features of Calvinism. In each instance the protest came from persons who were within the Reformed tradition. In each case the protest was based upon the Scriptures. Since the two movements, separated as they were by two centuries, were protesting against some of the same points of Calvinism, it followed that language similar to that used by Arminius and the Remonstrants was used in the Cumberland Presbyterian Confession of Faith. This similarity may be seen by comparing the statements of the two documents on the subject of prevenient grace. On this subject, Article IV of the Articles of the Remonstrants affirms:

> "That this grace of God is the beginning, the progress, and the end of all good; so that even the regenerate man can neither think, will nor effect any good, nor withstand any temptation to evil, without grace precedent (or prevenient), awakening, following and cooperating. So that all good deeds and all movements towards good that can be conceived in thought must be ascribed to the grace of God in Christ.
>
> "But with respect to the mode of operation, grace is not irresistible; for it is written of many that they resisted the Holy Spirit [Acts vii and elsewhere *passim*]."

On this same subject, the Cumberland Presbyterian Confession of Faith (sections 40 and 41) says this concerning the influence of the Holy Spirit moving upon the hearts of men:

> "This call of the Holy Spirit is purely of God's free grace alone, and not because of human merit, and is antecedent to all desire, purpose, and intention on the part of the sinner to come to Christ; so that while it is possible for all to be saved with it, none can be saved without it.
>
> "This call is not irresistible, but is effectual in those only who, in penitence and faith, freely surrender themselves wholly to Christ, the only name whereby men can be saved."

FROM PIETISM

There is yet another influence which has affected the character of the Cumberland Presbyterian Church. This is the movement known as pietism. In Germany in the seventeenth century faith had come to be regarded as "an assent by which you accept all articles of the faith" (Melanchthon). Emphasis had come to be laid almost entirely upon intellectual orthodoxy. In Lutheran circles, all that was expected of the layman was that he accept the dogmas of the Lutheran Church and partake of the sacraments. Pietism was born as a protest against these tendencies.

The pioneer in the pietist movement, Philipp Jakob Spener, was born in 1635. While attending the University of Strassburg, he became familiar with the discipline of biblical exegesis and saw in it an opportunity to instruct the people in the teachings of the Bible. When he became a pastor in Frankfurt, he sought to improve catechetical instruction in his parish. Beginning in 1670 he gathered together for periodic meetings a group of people who were interested in "spiritual things." This group would meet for Bible reading, prayer, and discussion of last Sunday's sermons. These meetings, as the movement spread, became known as *collegiae pietatis,* hence the term "pietism."

As measures for reform for the church, Spener advocated (1) gatherings of small groups for Bible reading and mutual helpfulness, (2) a better trained ministry, (3) experimental (experiential) knowledge of religion and a life befitting one's profession, the normal beginning of the Christian life being a conscious new birth, and (4) preaching designed to build up the Christian life rather than to exhibit the argumentative abilities of the preacher. If the heart was right, Spener believed, differences of intellectual interpretation were relatively unimportant.

On the doctrinal side, Spener taught that justification is preceded by repentance. The next step is saving faith. "Faith, which is inwrought by the Spirit of God, brings justification, adoption, and regeneration or new birth." Spener taught that the Christian should attain to perfection, not in an absolute sense, but in the sense of freedom from intentional sin. He also regarded salvation as "an experiential reality of which we can be assured by the witness of the Holy Spirit with our spirits." [5]

Another great leader of pietism in Germany was Hermann Francke. While teaching in the University of Leipzig, Francke experienced a new birth while writing a sermon on John 20:31. Then he stayed two months with Spener. Soon Francke was prohibited from holding conventicles, as these meetings of small groups were called, and therefore had to leave the university. He was made a professor, however, in the newly formed University at Halle, where he was joined by other pietists. Halle became a center of missionary activity. From here went Muhlenburg and other Lutheran ministers to organize the Lutherans who had migrated to America.

One of the most important results of the pietistic awakening has to do with the reconstitution of the Moravian Brethren under the leadership of Nicholas Zinzendorf (1700-1760), who had been brought up under pietistic influence at Halle and Wittenberg. The Hussites in Bohemia and Moravia were being subjected to persecution. In 1722, some of them drifted into Saxony, and Zinzendorf permitted them to settle on his estate where they founded the village of Herrnhut. In 1727, he assumed the task of their spiritual leadership. Here the Moravian Church was reconstituted, although Zinzendorf would have preferred that the Moravians become a *collegia pietatis* within the Saxon Lutheran state church.

The reconstituted Moravian Church launched a great missionary movement. Missions were attempted to the most difficult places: Guiana, Egypt, South Africa, and Labrador. It has been pointed out that while in the Protestant churches at large one person in five thousand becomes a missionary, the proportion among the Moravians has been one in sixty.

One who came under the influence of the Moravians was John Wesley, son of an Anglican clergyman and a devout mother. John's father founded a society similar to Spener's *collegiae pietatis* in Epworth in 1702. It was one of a large number of such societies in England. John was ordained a deacon in the Church of England in 1725, and in 1728 was ordained a priest. While attending Oxford University he and his brother Charles became members of a club which concerned itself with spiritual problems. Because they were so "methodical" in their efforts to work out their spiritual problems, someone called them "Methodists."

In 1735, John and Charles Wesley sailed for Oglethorpe's new colony of Georgia to be missionaries to the Indians. En route they fell into the company of a band of Moravians whose courage during a storm at sea greatly impressed John. Upon arriving in Georgia he met Spangenburg, head of the Moravian missionary work in America. "Do you know Jesus Christ?" Spangenburg asked Wesley. He answered, "I know He is the Saviour of the world." "True, but do you know He has saved you?" inquired Spangenburg. Wesley finally said he did, but afterward expressed fear that those were "vain words." [6]

After getting into difficulties in Georgia, John Wesley returned early in 1738 to England. Here he met another Moravian, Peter Bohler, who further instructed him. Then on Wednesday, May 24, 1738, after having gone "unwillingly" to an Anglican society in Aldersgate Street, he heard someone reading Luther's preface to his *Commentary on Romans*. "About a quarter before nine," writes Wesley, "while he (Luther) was describing the change which God works in the heart through faith in Christ, I felt my heart strangely warmed. I felt I did trust Christ, Christ alone, for salvation; and an assurance was given me that he had taken away my sins, even mine, and saved me from the law of sin and death." [7]

Wesley soon joined in the practice of field-preaching with George Whitefield, an Anglican evangelist later identified as a Methodist. As a result of their efforts a great revival occurred. Wesley organized his converts, not into churches, but into societies which in turn were divided into "classes" of about twelve members each. Wesley was Arminian in his theology. The Methodist movement has been called "Arminianism on fire."

Some time later, this same emphasis upon an experience of new birth was apparent in the preaching of James McGready in Kentucky. Like Wesley, McGready had entered the ministry before he had a true experience of new birth. He realized there were others in the church who were in the same condition. In his account of the beginning and progress of the revival in Kentucky, he tells us that he preached, as he was wont to do, the doctrines of "Regeneration, Faith, and Repentance." He states that frequently the question was asked him by some of his people, "Is Religion a sensible thing? If I were converted would I feel it, and know it?"

Is it surprising, then, that Methodists and the revivalistic Presbyterian ministers worked hand in hand in the "Great Revival" of the early 1800's? Later, a Methodist conference was the first Christian body to give official recognition to the Cumberland Presbytery following its organization in 1810.[8]

Pietism, with its emphasis on "heart religion," provided a basis upon which men could work together—a basis other than that of strict doctrinal agreement. It was this which Robert Donnell, one of the first generation of Cumberland Presbyterian ministers, must have had in mind when in arguing for open communion he said, "Christians feel alike, if they do not think alike." [9] It was this agreement of feeling which Philip William Otterbein experienced when, after hearing Martin Boehm preach, he made his way to the preacher and with overflowing heart exclaimed, "We are brethren." [10]

Insofar as the spirit of the Cumberland Presbyterian movement is concerned, its closest kinship is with groups which have been influenced by the pietists. In this regard it stands in much the same relation to the parent Presbyterian body as Methodists stand to their Anglican brethren. Cumberland Presbyterians from the beginning emphasized experimental (experiential) religion, a Christian life having its normal beginning in a conscious new birth. This was a major departure from the doctrine of unconditional election, traditionally regarded as the foundation stone upon which the doctrinal structure of Calvinism was built. Cumberland Presbyterians made the doctrine of the new birth the center of their doctrinal system.

SOMETHING TO THINK ABOUT

1. What are the distinguishing marks of the three main types of church government—congregational, episcopal, and presbyterian? What New Testament passages are usually cited in support of each?

2. The Lutheran churches and the Church of England took over much of the liturgy of the Roman Catholic Church, although they modified it in the light of Reformation doctrines and put it

into the language of the people. Presbyterians (as in the West-minster Confession) substituted general directions for worship for the liturgy. What do you think was gained or lost by abandoning the prayer book for the Directory for Worship?

3. Compare the Calvinist and Arminian positions on election.

4. What harmful effects did Arminius see as arising from the Calvinistic doctrine of unconditional election? Was his protest justified?

5. To what extent can a common Christian experience rather than a common body of doctrine be made the basis for Christian fellowship?

6. In what specific ways do Cumberland Presbyterians emphasize personal Christian experience? (See, for example, question II in the "Form of Church Covenant" and section 51 of the Constitution as found in the Confession of Faith.)

3. "A Mighty Rain"

" Revivalism, as a method of bringing religion to people out of touch with the churches, arose in the colonial period as a way of meeting a situation produced as a consequence of the great migrations of Europeans to the New World in the eighteenth century. The same conditions which produced it in the eighteenth century were reproduced again and again on every American frontier as people pushed westward across the continent. It was a way of bringing Christianity to individuals, and it stressed the fact that salvation depended upon individual decisions, that religion was a personal concern and not primarily an institutional matter." [1]

THE CUMBERLAND PRESBYTERIAN CHURCH had its beginning as a result of the Revival of 1800, as the western phase of the "second awakening" [2] is generally known. This revival had its beginning in Logan County, Kentucky, which was situated within an area earlier known as the Cumberland country.

THE CUMBERLAND COUNTRY

The territory known as the "Cumberland Country" originally comprised "that portion of Kentucky and Tennessee lying west of the Cumberland mountain; . . . extending northward to Green River in the former State, and southward indefinitely toward the Tennessee." [3] When the state line was run, that portion lying in Tennessee continued to be known as the Cumberland country, while that in Kentucky became known as the Green River country.

33

The first settlement in this area was made in 1780 at Nashville under the leadership of General James Robertson. Settlements had previously been made in northern Kentucky and in eastern Tennessee. Until 1799, when the first wagon road was opened from Knoxville to Nashville, the only overland route leading to the Cumberland country was a solitary Indian trail over which all supplies had to be transported by means of pack horses.

In 1800, Kentucky had a population of 220,955 persons, and Tennessee a population of 105,602. Both had recently attained statehood. Nashville, the principal town in the Cumberland country, had a population of 355 persons of whom 141 were slaves. The entire area was sparsely settled. Log cabins were the usual dwelling places of the frontiersmen, although a few frame houses had begun to appear. Furniture was simple and generally homemade.

RELIGIOUS SITUATION PRIOR TO THE REVIVAL

Following the War for Independence, religious conditions throughout the country generally were at a low ebb. Only about 10 per cent of the American people were church members, and many of these were only nominal Christians. The influence of the ideas which prompted the French Revolution had spread to the United States. Deism and freethinking had been popularized through wide distribution of Thomas Paine's *Age of Reason*. Lyman Beecher, who was a student at Yale College in 1795, describes the religious conditions in the college at that time. He writes:

> "The College was in a most ungodly state. The college church was almost extinct. Most of the students were skeptical, and rowdies were plenty. Wine and liquors were kept in many rooms; intemperance, profanity, gambling, and licentiousness were common." [4]

Beecher goes on to say that the boys called each other Voltaire, Rousseau, or D'Alembert. It is said that at Princeton in 1799, only three or four students "made any pretentions to piety." [5]

The prevalent indifference toward religion was accentuated in the West by the fact that the people were preoccupied with material things such as building their cabins and clearing their land for farming. Like the Jews in the days of the prophet Haggai, they built their own houses but neglected to build the house of God. "Powder and lead were in greater demand than books and stationery. The wants of the physical superseded those of the intellectual and moral man." [6] There was a scarcity of ministers of the gospel everywhere, but the lack of ministers was more acutely felt in the sparsely settled regions along the frontier.

There were, of course, devout church members who migrated to the West. Several denominations were represented among the settlers in Tennessee and Kentucky, but the Baptists, Methodists, and Presbyterians were predominant. The Reverend David Rice, the first Presbyterian minister to settle in Kentucky, moved to Mercer County from Virginia in 1783. In 1786, Transylvania Presbytery was organized. It included all of Kentucky, the Cumberland country of Tennessee, and reached north across the Ohio River. Also early to arrive in this region were the Baptist minister, who usually farmed for a living, and the Methodist circuit rider.

Although a few ministers were laboring faithfully, there is abundant evidence that the spiritual life of the Presbyterian churches in this region was at a low point. A considerable portion of the members had been received into the church without any experience of God's saving grace and without any understanding of the necessity for such an experience. As already noted, James McGready tells us that during his first year's ministry in Kentucky the members of his churches frequently asked him such questions as, "Is *Religion* a sensible thing? If I were converted would I feel it and know it?" On Finis Ewing's circuit, at a later date, it was common to hear people say, "I do all I can, and what I cannot do, Christ will do for me; if after I have done the best I can, I lack any thing, Christ must supply the balance." [7]

The reason for this situation is explained by one historian who observes that the preaching usually heard from Presbyterian pulpits in that section tended to "a dry, speculative orthodoxy, leaving the heart without interest, and the conscience without alarm." [8] That a Presbyterian minister in good standing could oppose the doctrines of faith, repentance, and regeneration with impunity, as actually happened soon after the commencement of the revival, does not argue well for the attitude of the Presbyterian ministry toward vital religion. The Reverend Samuel McSpadden, who lived in the Spring Hill community, near Nashville, has left the following testimony concerning the preaching of Dr. Thomas Craighead:

> "I sat under Dr. Craighead's preaching for fourteen or fifteen years, and never heard him advance any thing in favor of the new birth, evangelical repentance, or saving faith. . . . His sermons appeared to have not the slightest tendency to alarm the consciences of his hearers, or to render them dissatisfied with themselves. On the contrary, his preaching seemed calculated to quiet the fears of the people and keep them from becoming disturbed about their souls' salvation." [9]

He goes on to mention an instance of a woman, a member of Dr. Craighead's congregation, who, upon becoming alarmed concerning her spiritual state, went to Dr. Craighead for personal instruction. He assured her that all that was necessary for salvation was that she believe that Jesus Christ is the Son of God, and when she assented to this truth he told her she was already saved. She came away apparently satisfied but without having experienced any change of heart. Both Finis Ewing and his wife were, by their own statements, among those who united with Craighead's congregation without having experienced the new birth.

Dr. E. B. Crisman has argued that the system of doctrine held by the Presbyterian Church was a contributing factor to the spiritual deadness which prevailed. He points out that:

> ". . . the legitimate tendency of Calvinism is to a cold technical preaching, manifesting but a small amount of interest for the sinner's case. . . . The man who heartily believes the language of the Presbyterian Confession of Faith, chap. 3, sec. 3:—'By the decree of God, for the manifestation of his glory, some men and angels are predestinated unto everlasting life, and others foreordained to everlasting death,'—can have but little motive, and less room, to urge the necessity of salvation upon men promiscuously. For a physician to urge upon a patient the absolute necessity of a certain medicine for the healing of his disease, when that medicine cannot possibly be had, is not only foolish, but indicates a want of tender feeling in the physician. And for a preacher to urge upon

a sinner, the necessity of salvation in his case, when there is no salvation for him, is not only foolish and ungenerous, but it is trifling to an unwarranted extent, with the feelings of a fellow being, on the most solemn of all subjects. The man who believes the doctrine taught in the tenth chapter of the Presbyterian Confession—that God *will* convert the *elect* at his appointed and accepted time, and that men are altogether *passive* in their conversion—ought not to preach anything calculated to alarm the consciences of men, or urge them to immediate action." [10]

BEGINNINGS OF THE REVIVAL

The beginning of the "second awakening" was at Hampden-Sydney College, in Virginia, where it was largely a student movement.[11] Out of this early phase of the revival came a number of young ministers, several of whom became leaders in the Presbyterian Church in Kentucky and Tennessee.

The beginnings of the revival in Kentucky, however, took place under the ministry of James McGready. McGready was reared in North Carolina, and at the age of seventeen was admitted into the communion of the Presbyterian Church. As he was noted for his sobriety and strict morality, an uncle of his conceived the idea of preparing him for the ministry and sent him to the Reverend John McMillan's "Log College" in Pennsylvania. After he had been in college a year or two, he fell into the company of two "evangelical" Christians while visiting in the house of a friend. On retiring for the night the three men were all shown into the same room, McGready to one bed and the two friends to another. By and by, thinking McGready asleep, they proceeded to express to one another their views concerning his religious character, pronouncing him a mere formalist and a stranger to regenerating grace. McGready, however, being awake, heard all that was said, but instead of taking offense, he used the experience as an occasion for self-examination which resulted in his conviction that he was still a sinner. A few months later, he had a conversion experience. In 1789, he visited Hampden-Sydney College while the revival there was in progress. He was licensed to preach by the Redstone Presbytery, in Pennsylvania, but soon thereafter returned to North Carolina.

There he engaged faithfully in the task of warning sinners to flee from the wrath to come. Believing there were many in the church who were in the same condition as he himself had been, he devoted much attention to the unregenerate church member. He dwelt upon the necessity of the new birth and the importance of being able to tell the time when, and the place where, one was saved. So pungent were his messages that he encountered opposition. A letter was written to him in blood demanding that he leave the country, and a group of men assembled in his church on one occasion, tore down the seats, and burned the pulpit to ashes.

Soon after this occurrence, in consequence of a call from some of his former parishioners who had preceded him, he moved to Kentucky. He became pastor of the Red River Church in Logan County in the fall of 1796 and soon thereafter was instrumental in organizing the Gasper River and Muddy River churches, also in Logan County. Here he resumed the same kind of preaching as he had done in North Carolina emphasizing, as he himself tells us, the doctrines of "Regeneration, Faith, and Repentance." [12] Sensing the spiritual dearth existing in his churches, he encouraged the few spiritually-minded Christians to enter into covenant with him "to observe the third Saturday of each month, for one year, as a day of fasting and prayer, for the conversion of sinners in Logan county, and throughout the world" and "to spend one half hour every Saturday evening, beginning at the setting of the sun, and one half hour every Sabbath morning, at the rising of the sun, in pleading with God to revive his work." [13]

The first evidence of revival occurred in May, 1797, at Gasper River, when a woman, who had been a professor of religion and a member of the church, found her hope without foundation, was struck with deep conviction, and a few days later found peace and joy in believing. Immediately, she began visiting her friends and relatives, warning them of their danger and pleading with them to repent and seek the Lord. Her efforts were not in vain, for McGready testifies that for a time almost every sermon was used of God to the awakening of sinners. In the fall of 1797, a general decline was experienced, but the work was renewed in the summer of 1798 "at the administration of the sacrament of the supper, which was in July." The revival spread in 1798 to his other two churches, Muddy River and Red River. In the fall of 1798, the revival was checked for a time by the appearance of another Presbyterian minister who involved the churches in confusion and ridiculed the whole work of the revival.

In July, 1799, however, the work was renewed, and many were awakened and converted. The sacramental meetings, at Red River in July, at Gasper River in August, and at Muddy River in September, were all occasions when God's people were quickened and comforted and sinners awakened to a sense of their need. McGready records that, after a sermon by Mr. Rankin at Red River, "Presently several persons under deep conviction broke forth into a loud outcry—many fell to the ground, lay powerless, groaning, praying and crying for mercy."

SPREAD OF THE REVIVAL

In 1800, the revival spread beyond the bounds of McGready's congregations. Concerning the events of this year, McGready wrote, "Although many souls in these congregations, during the three preceding years, had been savingly converted, and now give living evidences of their union with Christ; yet all that work is only like a few drops before a mighty rain, when compared with the wonders of Almighty Grace, that took place in the year 1800."

During the sacramental meeting at Red River in June, 1800, multitudes were struck down under conviction, and ten persons were "savingly brought home to Christ." The sacramental meeting at Gasper River, in July, was a camp meeting. Multitudes came from distances of forty, fifty, and even a hundred miles. Some came from the Shiloh congregation, in Sumner County, Tennessee, which was being served by the Reverend William Hodge. Altogether, McGready estimated that forty-five souls were brought to Christ. The sacramental meeting at Muddy River, in August, resulted in the conversion of about fifty persons.

In the fall of 1800, doubtless as a result of the camp meeting in July, the revival spread to Ridge, Shiloh, and other places in Cumberland (i.e., Tennessee) as well as to other localities in Kentucky. McGready mentions other places, some as far away as the

Ohio River, to which the work of the revival had spread by 1801. It is also reported that in the spring of 1801, the Reverend Barton Stone, a Presbyterian minister from near Lexington, Kentucky, who, like McGready, had come from North Carolina, visited Mc-Gready's churches. Inspired by what he saw, Stone returned home and arranged for the Cane Hill camp meeting which, it is estimated, was attended by as many as twenty thousand persons.

METHODS USED

Concerning the revival, Sweet notes that "there arose in the west two distinct types of revivalism; the first was the Presbyterian-Congregational type, which might be termed a Calvinistic revivalism carried on under an educated leadership. This type insisted that the gospel be preached in all its Calvinistic purity; and that its appeal was intended only for those well grounded in the correct doctrines of Christianity. In the very nature of the case, this type of revivalism limited itself to the few which meant that the great majority of the people would be untouched and ignored. The second type of revivalism was the Baptist-Methodist-Disciple-Cumberland Presbyterian type, whose work was to bring Christianity to the great mass of religious illiterates. The first type offered salvation to the few; the second offered it to all. One was aristocratic in its appeal; the other democratic." [14] The emergence of the camp meeting indicates that the revivalism in the Cumberland country came to be definitely of the latter type.

At first the sacramental services were utilized in the fostering of the revival. The sacrament of the Lord's Supper was generally administered twice a year in the congregations which had regular pastors, and once a year in the vacant congregations. These sacramental meetings usually commenced on Friday and continued through Sunday. As the revival progressed, some of these meetings were protracted until Wednesday night.

The camp meeting grew out of the sacramental meeting. According to one account, the camp meeting had its beginning in the fact that a family recently come from one of the Carolinas came in their wagon to the sacramental meeting at Gasper River (in 1799) and camped on the ground. At another meeting, two or three families camped on the ground. In each case, these families were among those most richly blessed. McGready, observing what had happened, announced that the sacramental meeting at Gasper River in July, 1800, would be a camp meeting and sent pressing invitations to ministers at a distance to come and see the strange work which was taking place and to encourage as many of their people as possible to attend. Widely separated as were the settlements, the camp meeting afforded an opportunity for many to hear the gospel who otherwise would not have been reached. Those who camped on the ground were relatively free from worldly cares and were able to center their attention upon spiritual things.

At that period it was not customary to have the penitent separate themselves from the congregation by coming to an altar for prayer. The "anxious-seat," or "mourner's bench," had not as yet been introduced. Those who were affected by the preaching of the gospel were left to struggle with their convictions until, like the multitude on the day of Pentecost, they were constrained to cry out, "Brethren, what shall we do?" or until, overcome by conflicting emotions, they fell prostrate upon the ground. At times so many were stricken down that cries for mercy and the personal instruction of those who were convicted of their sin went on throughout the night.

It should be recognized that the methods employed during the revival were at that time new methods. As will be seen in the following chapter, the use of methods which by some were regarded as unorthodox was one factor which got the leaders of the revival into trouble. These methods served well to make possible the communication of the gospel in the situation which then existed. It goes without saying that other methods may be better employed in communicating the gospel in the period and social milieu in which we live. We will do well, however, to emulate the concern for people which motivated those men of the frontier to employ extraordinary measures to take the gospel to the widely scattered inhabitants of the old Southwest. Having such concern, we must seek to discover the most effective methods of communicating the gospel in the age in which we live.

EVALUATION OF THE REVIVAL

From the beginning there was opposition to the revival. Some of those who opposed were avowed unbelievers, while others were professors of religion. The latter group included several ministers of the gospel. Some who were sticklers for order became alarmed at some of the unusual occurrences at the sacramental meetings.

There had been opposition to the revivals in North Carolina before McGready came to Kentucky. The Reverend James Smith tells us that because of McGready's plain, heart-searching messages and his insistence upon the necessity of regeneration, "The cry was raised against him, he is running the people distracted, diverting their attention from their necessary avocations; and creating in the minds of decent, orderly, moral people, unnecessary alarm about the eternal destiny of their souls." [15]

In writing about the opposition to revivals in North Carolina, Dr. T. C. Anderson has stated:

> "The existence of two parties may be traced back in the history of the Church for centuries. Perhaps they are coeval with the prevalence of revivals; for whenever and wherever an extensive and gracious revival prevails, that portion of the Church under its influence will become more spiritual in their devotions, and energetic in efforts for the promotion of religion, than those portions of the Church, which have not participated in the revival. Then the active party, forgetting their former coldness and apathy, may be disposed to censure those who now manifest the same listlessness and inactivity which they themselves had recently indulged. And the lukewarm will be sure to look upon the newborn zeal of the revival party as the offspring of fanaticism, rather than an increase of spirituality. This want of charity and forbearance will originate distrust, opposition, and strife." [16]

In order to render a just appraisal of any revival, one must look to the permanent results in the life and character of its subjects. McGready himself stated that "among the great numbers in our country that professed to obtain religion, I scarcely know an instance of any that gave a comfortable ground of hope to the people of God, that they had religion, and have been admitted to the privileges of the church, that have, in any degree, disgraced their profession, or given us any ground to doubt their religion." [17]

The Reverend James Smith, writing in about the year 1835, says,

> "Indeed, if we may judge of the great mass of the converts of the revival by those who yet live, they were a humble, intelligent, and evangelical body of Christians, who were blessed with clear views of the truth as it is in Jesus, and were ready for every good word and work." [18]

George Addison Baxter, a young Presbyterian minister who in the summer or fall of 1801 took a long horseback ride from Virginia to Kentucky to see the strange work which was going on, has left the following testimony:

> "On my way to Kentucky, I was told by settlers on the road, that the character of Kentucky travelers was entirely changed, and that they were now as distinguished for sobriety, as they had formerly been for dissoluteness; and, indeed, I found Kentucky the most moral place I had ever been in; a profane expression was hardly heard, a religious awe seemed to pervade the country, and some deistical characters had confessed that, from whatever cause the revival might originate, it made the people better." [19]

The same writer goes on to say,

> ". . . Upon the whole, sir, I think the revival in Kentucky among the most extraordinary that have ever visited the Church of Christ; and, all things considered, peculiarly adapted to the circumstances of that country. Infidelity was triumphant, and religion at the point of expiring; something of an extraordinary nature seemed necessary to arrest the attention of a giddy people, who were ready to conclude that Christianity was a fable, and futurity a dream. This revival has done it; it has confounded infidelity, awed vice into silence, and brought numbers, beyond calculation, under serious impressions." [20]

The revival did indeed serve both as a uniting and a dividing factor. On the one hand, Christians of different denominations, especially Methodists and Presbyterians, labored together in the revival. A notable example of this is the presence of the Reverend John McGee, a Methodist minister, at one of McGready's sacramental meetings. On the other hand, the revival resulted in the separation of two different groups from the Presbyterian Church: One, under the leadership of Barton Stone, who became dissatisfied with the Presbyterian system of doctrine, went out to form the Springfield Presbytery. This body later dissolved for the members to call themselves simply "Christians" and to reject all man-made creeds. Stone himself, and many of his followers, later joined hands with Alexander Campbell and his followers to form the Disciples of Christ. The other group which separated from the Presbyterian Church organized the Cumberland Presbytery in 1810.

SOMETHING TO THINK ABOUT

1. What circumstances contributed to the low estate of religion in Kentucky and Tennessee near the end of the eighteenth century?

2. Of what significance is the fact that the "second awakening" began as a student movement?

3. What effect did McGready's own experience have upon his preaching?

4. What part did (1) preaching, (2) personal testimony, and (3) worship (e.g., communion) play in the furtherance of the Revival of 1800?

5. William Warren Sweet has noted that in the west there were two types of revivalism, one which appealed to those who were well grounded in the correct doctrines of Christianity, and another which appealed to the great mass of religious illiterates. Which type is your local church following in its evangelistic efforts?

6. What were some values of the camp meeting as a means of evangelism?

7. How do you account for the fact that the means used in the revival were opposed by some Presbyterian ministers?

8. How do you account for the fact that the Revival of 1800 resulted both in co-operation between denominations and in divisions which resulted in the formation of other denominations?

4. A New Church Is Born

THE SPREAD OF the revival resulted in an unprecedented demand for the preaching of the gospel in the scattered settlements on the frontier. Persons whose families had been blessed through attending the camp meetings at a distance from their homes desired that the gospel be preached within their own settlements. McGready mentions vacant congregations far removed from any organized church and served only by occasional supply preachers. The Letter of the Council of Revival Ministers to the General Assembly of 1807 recalls that "Unable to resist the pressing solicitations from every quarter for preaching, with unutterable pleasure we went out, laboring day and night, until our bodies were worn down, and after all we could not supply one-third of the places calling on us for preaching."

In the midst of this dearth of ministers the Reverend David Rice, the venerable father of Presbyterianism in Kentucky, suggested to the leaders in the revival movement in the Cumberland-Logan County area during the year of 1801 that they enlist the help of laymen who seemed disposed to exercise their gifts in public exhortation, even though those laymen had not attained the standard of education prescribed by the Constitution of the Presbyterian Church. The Presbyterian "Form of Government" recommends that prior to licensure a candidate for the ministry have a college education or its equivalent and a knowledge of the Latin language and the original languages in which the Scriptures were written, and that "no candidate, except in extraordinary cases, be

45

licensed, unless, after his having completed the usual course of academical studies, he shall have studied divinity at least two years, under some approved divine or professor of theology." [1] Persons of such qualifications were not to be found in the West in the early 1800's in sufficient numbers to meet the pressing demand for ministers.

PRESBYTERY ACTS TO MEET A NEED

At the meeting of Transylvania Presbytery in October, 1801, four men—Finis Ewing, Alexander Anderson, Samuel King, and Ephraim McLean—offered themselves to presbytery for the service of the church and were licensed to exhort and catechize. Texts were also assigned them on which they were to prepare discourses to be read at the next session of presbytery. At the next meeting of presbytery, in the spring of 1802, Anderson was received as a candidate for the ministry by a majority of one vote while the others were rejected by a majority of one vote. In the fall of 1802, however, Transylvania Presbytery licensed Anderson, Ewing, and King to preach the gospel, the presbytery considering their cases as coming under the head of the "extraordinary cases" provided for in the "Form of Government." This action of presbytery did not go unchallenged, for three ministers and two elders, led by the Reverend Thomas B. Craighead, registered their dissent.

On October 14, 1802, just six days after the licensure of these three men by Transylvania Presbytery, the first session of the Synod of Kentucky was convened, two new presbyteries having been carved out of Transylvania Presbytery. At its first meeting the Synod of Kentucky divided Transylvania Presbytery again by creating Cumberland Presbytery out of its southwestern portion. This presbytery held its first meeting at Ridge Church, in Tennessee, in April, 1803.

Cumberland Presbytery had ten ordained ministers in its original membership. Five of them—James McGready, William Hodge, William McGee, John Rankin, and Samuel McAdow—were leaders in the promotion of the revival. The other five—Thomas B. Craighead, Terah Templin, John Bowman, Samuel Donnell, and James Balch—were equally zealous in their opposition to the revival. At the first meeting of Cumberland Presbytery, the revivalists were strengthened by the addition of the Reverend James Haw. According to the minutes of Cumberland Presbytery, he had been received from the Republican Methodist Church at the preceding meeting of Transylvania Presbytery, and, since he lived within the bounds of the newly organized Cumberland Presbytery, he was invited to take his seat as a member thereof.

At its first meeting, Cumberland Presbytery provided for an intermediate session for the ordination of Alexander Anderson.[2] At the next regular meeting, in the fall of 1803, an order was passed for the ordination of Finis Ewing at an intermediate session of presbytery. At the regular spring meeting in 1804, the first after his ordination, the legality of Ewing's ordination was called in question, but the presbytery voted by a large majority to seat him. At this same meeting, provision was made for the ordination of Samuel King at an intermediate session of presbytery. James Porter, who at a previous meeting had passed an examination on the languages, was licensed. Meanwhile, several other men had been received as candidates for the ministry, while still others had been licensed to exhort and catechize. During 1804, the revival party suffered the loss of Alexander Anderson by death.

A DOCTRINAL ISSUE IS RAISED

At the meeting of the Synod of Kentucky in October, 1804, a letter was received from the Reverend Thomas B. Craighead and others in which reference was made to the licensures and ordinations recently performed by Cumberland Presbytery. This letter was in the nature of a "common fame" letter; that is to say, the writers did not propose themselves to substantiate the allegations made, but submitted them only as circulating rumors which ought to be investigated. In addition to raising the question of the educational qualifications of the men who had been licensed and ordained, it was reported that Cumberland Presbytery had required the men thus licensed and ordained to adopt the Confession of Faith only insofar as they deemed it agreeable with the Word of God. In a later discussion before a synodical commission, it was argued by the commission that no one could know what these men believed in matters of doctrine, and it was suggested that one could as easily adopt the Koran in the same manner. On the other hand, the members of Cumberland Presbytery contended that the fact that the men adopted the Confession of Faith at all was evidence that they regarded it as the best of all human creeds, and that the real difficuly had arisen over the idea of fatality which seemed to be taught in the Confession under "the mysterious doctrine of predestination."

That the "young men" had a right to state their scruples regarding the Westminster Confession, and that the presbytery, being the judge of their soundness in the faith, had the right to license and ordain them notwithstanding their scruples, is apparent from a consideration of the Adopting Act, by which Presbyterian ministers in the first synod in America were required to subscribe to the Westminster Confession. The Adopting Act contained the following provision:

> ". . . And in case any minister of this synod, or any candidate for the ministry, shall have any scruple with respect to any article or articles of said Confession or Catechisms, he shall, at the time of his making said declaration, declare his sentiments to the presbytery or synod, who shall, notwithstanding, admit him to the exercise of the ministry within our bounds, and to ministerial communion, if the synod or presbytery shall judge his scruples to be only about articles not essential and necessary in doctrine, worship, or government. But if the synod, or presbytery, shall judge such ministers or candidates erroneous in essential and necessary articles of faith, the synod or presbytery shall declare them incapable of communion with them. And the synod do solemnly agree that none of us will traduce or use any opprobrious terms of those that differ from us in these extra-essential and not necessary points of doctrine, but treat them with the same friendship, kindness and brotherly love as if they had not differed from us in such sentiments."

In consequence of the "common fame" letter, the synod cited all parties involved to appear before the next meeting of synod and appointed a committee of five to attend the earliest meeting of Cumberland Presbytery and report their observations to the synod at its next meeting. Only one member of this committee attended Cumberland Presbytery, however, and he made no report to synod.

At the spring meeting of Cumberland Presbytery, 1805, provision was made for an intermediate session of presbytery for the ordination of William Dickey and for another for the ordination of Samuel Hodge and Thomas Nelson. The meeting for the ordination of Mr. Dickey was attended only by members of the anti-revival party, while the meeting for the ordination of Nelson and Hodge was attended only by members of the revival party.

A SYNODIC COMMISSION TAKES
UNPRECEDENTED MEASURES

At the meeting of the Synod of Kentucky in the fall of 1805, the minutes of Cumberland Presbytery were before the synod for the first time. The committee appointed to examine these minutes was extremely critical. The records were said to be defective and the history in some places obscure. The seating of James Haw without his having recanted his Methodist sentiments, the licensure of persons to exhort, and the licensure of Farr, "an illiterate man," were called in question. Furthermore, attention was called to the phrase "Finis Ewing's Circuit," which apparently was not considered an orthodox Presbyterian term. The result was the appointment of a commission "vested with full Synodical powers to confer with the Members of Cumberland Presbytery and to adjudicate upon their Presbyterial proceedings which appear upon the Minutes of said Presbytery for the purpose aforesaid and taken notice of by the Committee appointed by Synod to examine said Minutes." The commission was also instructed to take into consideration and decide upon the letter from the Reverend Thomas B. Craighead and others and upon an appeal from the judgment of Cumberland Presbytery by certain members of the Shiloh congregation. The Shiloh church had become divided over the revival, and the anti-revival group had been trying in vain to be recognized by the presbytery.

The commission met at Gasper River meeting house, Logan County, Kentucky, December 3-10, 1805. Early in its proceedings it decided that Cumberland Presbytery had acted illegally in receiving James Haw without examining him on divinity or requiring him to adopt the Confession of Faith of the Presbyterian Church. The charge that the presbytery had licensed and ordained men contrary to the rules and discipline of the Presbyterian Church was then taken up with special attention being given to the matter of the presbytery's requiring only a partial adoption of the Confession of Faith. The commission therefore resolved to examine "those persons irregularly licensed and irregularly ordained by Cumberland Presbytery and judge of their qualifications for the Gospel Ministry."

At this point the majority of Cumberland Presbytery, through the Reverend William Hodge as their spokesman, refused to submit to the foregoing resolution on the ground that they, as a presbytery, had the exclusive privilege of examining and licensing their own candidates and that synod had no right to take the business out of their hands. The commission then addressed the demand for re-examination directly to the men involved. The majority of the members of Cumberland Presbytery requested permission to leave the meeting temporarily.[3] Upon their return, each of the older members of Cumberland Presbytery—McGready, Hodge, McGee, Rankin, and McAdow—was called up individually and asked, "Do you submit? or not submit?" Each refused to submit. Likewise the persons allegedly "irregularly licensed" and "irregularly ordained" by Cumberland Presbytery refused to submit with the exception of two who requested more time. Subsequently they, too, refused to submit to the commission's demand.

The commission then declared that the young men who refused to submit to re-examination had never had any regular authority from Cumberland Presbytery to preach the gospel. This action of the commission prohibited those who refused re-examination from exhorting, preaching, and administering ordinances in consequence of any authority they had obtained from Cumberland Presbytery "until they submit to our jurisdiction, and undergo the requisite examination." Those who were absent, together with James Haw, were laid under the same prohibition. The five older ministers were cited to appear at the annual session of the

Synod of Kentucky for not submitting to the examination of the
younger men; and William Hodge, William McGee, and John
Rankin were charged with holding and propagating doctrines contrary to those contained in the Confession of Faith of the Presbyterian Church and were cited to appear before the Synod of
Kentucky to answer to these charges.

Although the commission seems to have relied almost exclusively on the "common fame" letter written the year before
by Craighead and others, rather than upon the minutes of Cumberland Presbytery, the commission concluded its action on these
particular difficulties with the following resolution: "Resolved
also that the Revd. Thos. B. Craighead and, Samuel Donald and
John Bowman, have acted irregularly in taking up the case on
fama clamora and not by dissent." In other words, the information
on which the commission relied mainly for its agenda was acknowledged to have been brought before the synod in an irregular
manner.

It is true that synod, under the Presbyterian "Form of Government," has the power "to review the records of presbyteries,
and approve or censure them; to redress whatever has been done
by presbyteries contrary to order; to take effectual care that presbyteries observe the constitution of the Church." To the presbytery, on the other hand, is given the power "to examine and license
candidates for the holy ministry; to ordain, install, remove, and
judge ministers." Thus, neither the commission nor the Synod of
Kentucky itself had the right to require those men who had been
examined, licensed, and ordained by Cumberland Presbytery to
stand another examination before Synod.

The Synod of Kentucky, at its next meeting, in October,
1806, dissolved Cumberland Presbytery and attached its members
to Transylvania Presbytery. It also suspended William Hodge and
John Rankin after trying in vain "to reclaim them to a due sense
of the authority of Synod and submission to the order and discipline of the Church."

ATTEMPTS AT RECONCILIATION FAIL

Soon after the synodic commission had done its work, the

revival ministers of Cumberland Presbytery consulted together and resolved to form themselves into a council. In this capacity they met regularly for mutual encouragement but refrained from transacting any presbyterial business. The older members of the presbytery agreed to continue preaching and administering the ordinances as formerly and encouraged the "young men" to continue their ministerial functions also.

In 1807 the council directed a letter to the General Assembly of the Presbyterian Church in which a full history of their case was set forth and a redress of their grievances requested. The General Assembly addressed a letter to the Synod of Kentucky in which the opinion was expressed that some of the proceedings relative to Cumberland Presbytery were "of at least questionable regularity." The Assembly suggested to the synod that it ought to review some of its actions and possibly modify them in some respects. Especially called in question were the proceedings of synod requiring the young men "irregularly licensed and ordained" to be given up to the synod for examination, suspending the "irregularly ordained ministers" without process, and suspending Hodge and Rankin for not submitting to the examination of the young men. The synod did review its proceedings, but by an overwhelming vote reaffirmed all of its previous actions. The synod addressed a communication to the General Assembly explaining its position. Somehow this letter failed to reach the next Assembly, so a second letter was sent at the direction of the synod in the fall of 1808.

Meanwhile, Transylvania Presbytery, to which the matter of the members of the former Cumberland Presbytery had been referred for settlement, took action in October, 1808, inviting Hodge, McGready, McGee, McAdow, and Rankin to come to the next regular meeting of presbytery at Glasgow for a friendly interview. They were invited to bring along with them as many of the men who had been declared by the commission to be destitute of authority to preach the gospel as they might deem proper. William Hodge appeared in behalf of the brethren of the former Cumberland Presbytery, and after a conference with him the presbytery agreed to write him and his brethren a letter stating on what terms a reconciliation might be effected. The letter as transmitted to Mr. Hodge a few days later stated that Hodge's restoration "can only be effected by a proper acknowledgement of the faith & submission to the authority of our church as contained in our book of discipline to which you are referred." The same, it was stated, would apply to the other brethren who were yet under citation for not submitting to the authority of synod. With regard to the "young men," a "formal examination of them respecting doctrine & discipline" was regarded as indispensable, as was also "an unequivocal adoption of our Confession of Faith." It is worthy of notice that nothing was said at this point concerning literary attainments.

The General Assembly which met in 1809 received both letters which had been sent by the Synod of Kentucky and likewise the records of synod, which had not been sent up the preceding year. The interests of the synod were also represented by the Reverend John Lyle, who had served as a member of the synodic commission in 1805. One Presbyterian historian recounts that at first Lyle was overawed in the presence of the Presbyterian divines whose names the people on the frontier were accustomed to pronounce with veneration, but that at last "having overcome his awe, and yielding to his feelings as was his wont, wept freely as he portrayed in vivid colors the probable effects of the discomfiture and disgrace of the friends of truth and order." [4] The General Assembly accepted the explanations of the synod and gave it a vote of thanks. There was no further opportunity for the revival ministers to obtain a redress of their grievances at the General Assembly level.

The council, however, determined to make one more effort toward reconciliation. Two commissioners were appointed to convey to the Synod of Kentucky or to Transylvania Presbytery the decision that the ministers belonging to the council, both old and young, licensed and ordained, were willing to be examined by presbytery or synod upon two conditions. The first was that they be received or rejected as a connected body, and that if received, their authority formerly derived from Cumberland Presbytery be recognized. The other was that if they had to adopt the Confession of Faith, they be permitted to do so "with the exception of fatality only." William Hodge attended the meeting of Kentucky Synod, but instead of carrying out the council's instructions, he requested that provision be made for his own restoration. His request was referred to Transylvania Presbytery, which was directed to meet on December 6.

The council met again on the fourth Tuesday in October to ascertain the results of Mr. Hodge's efforts. He stated that he thought the synod had complied with the substance of the council's request, but after comparing the minutes of the previous meeting of the council with the petition Mr. Hodge had presented to synod, the council thought otherwise. The council then voted to constitute into a presbytery. At this point William Hodge, his nephew, Samuel Hodge, and Thomas Nelson withdrew. James McGready had not met with the council for some time. Rankin had joined the Shakers. This left only three ordained ministers present: Finis Ewing, Samuel King, and William McGee. McGee could not get the consent of his mind to proceed with the organization of a presbytery at this time. Consequently the council adjourned to meet at the Ridge Meetinghouse on the third Tuesday in March, 1810, after agreeing that each member should be released from his bond unless previous to that time three ordained ministers belonging to the body should have constituted a presbytery.

At the meeting of Transylvania Presbytery on December 6, William Hodge appeared, expressed sorrow for past irregularities, agreed to submit to the authority and discipline of the Presbyterian Church, and declared his unequivocal adoption of and adherence to the Confession of Faith. He was restored to the full exercise of all the functions of the gospel ministry and seated as a member of presbytery. At the same time, Thomas Nelson and Samuel Hodge, both of whom had been ordained by Cumberland Presbytery, expressed their desire to submit themselves to the wisdom and determination of the presbytery. After having examined them "so far as was thought expedient" and having secured their acceptance of the Confession of Faith, the presbytery recognized their licensure and ordination.

A NEW PRESBYTERY IS ORGANIZED

Following the adjournment of the council in October, Ewing in particular exerted himself toward securing the organization of a presbytery. In a letter to James Porter, one of the licentiates under the care of the council, he indicated his willingness to proceed with only two ordained ministers; however, he was spared this necessity. On February 2, 1810, Ewing and King visited another licentiate, Ephraim McLean, who had been among the first to offer himself to Transylvania Presbytery for the service of the church. McLean agreed to accompany them to the home of Samuel McAdow in Dickson County, Tennessee. Late the next afternoon they arrived at McAdow's house and laid before him the proposal to constitute a presbytery. McAdow would not take so drastic a step without first seeking divine guidance. The next morning, after a night spent in prayer, McAdow informed the group of his readiness to join with them in constituting a presbytery. So on February 4, 1810, in the home of Samuel McAdow, three ministers—Finis Ewing, Samuel King, and Samuel McAdow —constituted a presbytery to be known as Cumberland Presbytery, after which they ordained McLean to the full work of the ministry and adjourned to meet at Ridge Meetinghouse on the third Tuesday in March.

It was not the intention of those who constituted this presbytery to start a new denomination. They still hoped for a reunion with the Synod of Kentucky or some other synod of the Presbyterian Church. After their efforts in this direction had been rebuffed, however, provision was made in 1813 for the organization of two other presbyteries, Elk and Logan, and in October of that year the Cumberland Synod held its first session at Beech Church, Sumner County, Tennessee. In 1829, a General Assembly was formed.

WHY A NEW CHURCH?

Why did the difficulties arising between the Synod of Kentucky and the revival ministers in Cumberland Presbytery terminate as they did? What were the factors which seemed to necessitate the formation of a new presbytery?

The chief difficulty was *not* ministerial education. Although the difficulties had their beginning in the decision of Transylvania Presbytery, and subsequently Cumberland Presbytery, to make use of the provision for "extraordinary cases" in order to obtain a more adequate supply of ministers, the question of education virtually dropped out of the picture before the difficulties issued in the organization of the new presbytery. Thus, when Transylvania Presbytery, in the spring of 1809, wrote to the Reverend William Hodge stating the terms on which he and his co-laborers could be restored to good standing in the presbytery, the educational qualifications of the "young men" were not even mentioned. Only submission to the authority of the church and unequivocal adoption of the Confession of Faith were required. Dr. Davidson, a Presbyterian historian, says, "It was not the want of classical learning, but *unsoundness in doctrine,* the adoption of the Confession with *reservations,* . . . that created the grand difficulty; and the removal of this hindrance would have wonderfully facilitated the accommodation of the other."[5]

Both the doctrinal issue (the insistence on the part of the Synod of Kentucky and Transylvania Presbytery that the "young men" must accept the Confession of Faith unequivocally) and the persistent demand for submission played a large part in the final issue. There were men who, like Finis Ewing, simply would not accept that which they could not preach with a clear conscience. On the other hand, the synod continued to demand submission as the price of restoration. Dr. Cossitt suggests "that the Kentucky Synod, finding that they had been misled by Craighead, Balch, and Bowman, as well as their own prejudice and party spirit, to the adoption of unauthorized measures which even the General Assembly had censured, as being 'at least of questionable regularity,' deemed the submission of the young men to their wrong measures indispensable to the justification of their Commission's proceedings."[6] The submission of the young men would have been the best means of forestalling any critical investigation of the acts of the synod and of its commission.

Underlying all these difficulties one fact seems apparent. The revival ministers were willing to adapt themselves and their standards to the situation in which they were laboring. It was this willingness to adapt their standards to the circumstances which led the revival ministers to make use of the provision for "extraordinary cases" and bring into the ministry some who did not have a classical education. It was also their willingness to use new methods which led to the employment of camp meetings and circuit preaching as means of reaching the people in the widely scattered settlements on the frontier. As the revival spread, some of the participants came to realize that the "old wineskins" of a theological system which taught unconditional election and reprobation could not contain the "new wine" of personal experiences which led the multitudes to cry out, "Men and brethren, what shall we do?"

SOMETHING TO THINK ABOUT

1. Would it have been possible to meet the need for ministers in the Presbyterian Church on the frontier without relaxing the educational standards to some degree? Is it possible today to meet the needs of Cumberland Presbyterian churches through seminary trained men alone? Give reasons for your answers.

2. What precedent was there in the Presbyterian Church for allowing the young men who were being licensed or ordained to accept the Confession of Faith with reservations?

3. In what ways did the commission of Kentucky Synod overstep its authority?

4. What points of difference seemingly made reconciliation between Kentucky Synod and the ministers of Cumberland Presbytery impossible?

5. How would you explain to an inquirer the events and causes which led to the organization of the Cumberland Presbyterian Church?

6. In what respects did the founders of the Cumberland Presbyterian Church prove their willingness to make adaptations to meet the needs of the frontier?

7. Evaluate the viewpoints of the pro-revival party and the anti-revival party of the first Cumberland Presbytery.

5. Advancing with the Frontier

EVEN BEFORE EWING, King, and McAdow met to organize Cumberland Presbytery, missionary work was being attempted far beyond the bounds of the churches in the area where the revival had its origin. In 1807 the Council sent Robert Bell to the new settlements near what is now Huntsville, Alabama. The next year Thomas Calhoun was sent to this field, and in 1809, Robert Donnell. Donnell was traveling and preaching in Alabama when news reached him of the organization of the new Cumberland Presbytery.

FROM THE REORGANIZATION OF CUMBERLAND PRESBYTERY TO THE ORGANIZATION OF THE GENERAL ASSEMBLY

The method of circuit preaching was continued under the new presbytery. The minutes of the second meeting of presbytery mention the "lower circuit" or Livingston circuit, "Elk River Circuit," "Nashville Circuit," and the "upper circuit." A year later the "Logan circuit" is mentioned, and the mouth of Green River was to be visited by McLean, Harris, Chapman, and whoever rode the lower circuit. The minutes of presbytery for November, 1812, contain the following:

> "Ordered, that Mr. John Carnahan form a circuit on the Arkansaw in the bounds of those settlements in which he lives, and report to Presbytery his success when he returns."

The minutes of Cumberland Presbytery (1810-1813) mention thirty-seven churches or societies. Most of these were organized after the formation of the new presbytery.

As soon as the synod was organized, each of the three presbyteries—Elk, Logan, and Nashville—accepted the task of cultivating the vast fields which were open to it. Elk Presbytery included within its field of operations both Alabama and Arkansas. Logan Presbytery extended its bounds to include Illinois, Indiana, and Ohio. East Tennessee and West Tennessee came within the jurisdiction of Nashville Presbytery. Both Elk and Logan had a part in evangelizing Missouri. That was just at the time when most of the territories mentioned were being opened up for settlement. That part of Tennessee and Kentucky west of the Tennessee River was purchased from the Indians in 1819. The first territorial legislature in Alabama assembled in 1817. Illinois was made a state in 1818. Arkansas was organized as a territory in 1819. Missouri, which had been organized as a territory in 1812, became a state in 1821 by virtue of the famous Missouri Compromise.

Concerning the plan of the presbyteries for cultivating these fields McDonnold says:

"The plan which all the presbyteries fell upon was three-fold. All the vast fields under their care were districted, and itinerants sent to each district. These itinerants established circuits of preaching places, and made appointments for preaching every day in the week. This was generally missionary work, outside of all organized congregations. If the missionary could collect enough members to organize a church, he took their names, pledging them to form a church as soon as an ordained preacher could be had to organize them. The missionary was not usually an ordained minister. This was the first branch of the system.

"The second branch pertained to organized congregations. In these the presbytery appointed sacramental meetings semi-annually, and designated the preachers who were to officiate. The fall meetings were camp-meetings, as well as sacramental, and every ordained preacher, no matter what his pastoral relations might be, was required to attend these camp-meetings during the fall months, and was also required to perform his part of that other work on the circuits which unordained men could not do. The presbytery, at every session, designated what portion of these duties fell to the lot of each ordained minister, and each was held to rigid account for his fidelity to the work assigned to him.

"The third branch of the system consisted of such features of regular pastorates as could be made consistent with the two preceding branches. In the orders of these presbyteries I find it no uncommon thing for a so-called pastor of this period to be required, in the course of a year, to attend as many as a dozen sacramental meetings, distant from fifty to three hundred miles from his home; and when called on to report at the next meeting of the presbytery, it was a rare thing for anyone to report a failure. When failure was reported, the reasons were investigated." [1]

Just what was involved in "riding a circuit" in those days may be illustrated from a journal kept by W. A. Scott while he was a licentiate under the care of Hopewell Presbytery. He was appointed in the fall of 1830 to a circuit which included Carroll, Henry, Weakley, Gibson, and Obion Counties, in West Tennessee. He had thirty regular preaching places, and it took him five weeks to make the round. He managed to have a sabbath appointment on each round at each of three county seat towns: Paris, Dresden, and Huntingdon. There were organized churches at Bethel (Mc-Lemoresville), Shiloh, and probably at Meridian and Mt. Pleasant. The rest of the appointments seem to have been in private homes. At the time of his appointment to this circuit, Scott was not quite eighteen years of age.[2]

The progress of missionary work during the period of the synod can be traced in part through the organization of new presbyteries. In 1819 the ladies' missionary society at Russellville, Kentucky, made possible the sending of R. D. Morrow as a missionary to Missouri at a salary of twenty dollars per month. Green P. Rice had preached at St. Louis as early as 1817, and Daniel Buie, another Cumberland Presbyterian minister, had moved to Missouri sometime prior to Morrow's first visit in 1819. In the fall of that year the order was passed for the organization of McGee Presbytery which had as its original members Green P. Rice, Daniel Buie, R. D. Morrow, and John Carnahan. Its territory consisted of Arkansas, Missouri, and western Illinois.

In 1821 the synod divided Elk Presbytery by creating two new presbyteries, Alabama and Tennessee. At the same meeting Anderson Presbytery was created out of Logan Presbytery and Lebanon out of Nashville. In 1822, Illinois Presbytery was formed out of parts of Anderson and McGee Presbyteries, for Green P. Rice had already organized the Bear Creek Church near the present site of Greenville, Illinois, and D. W. McLin had organized the Hopewell church (later called Enfield) in White County.

In 1825 Alabama Presbytery was dissolved and a part of its members, together with two ministers from Tennessee Presbytery, were appointed to constitute the Bigby Presbytery. The remainder of the members of Alabama Presbytery were attached to Tennessee Presbytery. At the same meeting McGee Presbytery was divided to form the Arkansas Presbytery, which held its first meeting at the house of John Craig in Independence County, Arkansas.

Early in its history Logan Presbytery had two districts, Wabash and Indiana, to which missionaries were regularly sent. In 1821 this territory became a part of Anderson Presbytery. In 1825 Anderson Presbytery was divided to form Indiana Presbytery.

As early as 1815, Thomas Calhoun and Robert Donnell made a missionary tour through East Tennessee but did not attempt to organize any churches. In 1818 David Foster was ordered by Nashville Presbytery to a regular circuit in East Tennessee, and in 1823 J. S. Guthrie and Abner Lansden were sent to that field. They were joined the following year by George Donnell and S. M. Aston. The synod in 1827 ordered the organization of Knoxville Presbytery.

In 1820, less than a year after the purchase of West Tennessee from the Indians, John L. Dillard and James McDonnold were sent to that country. In 1821, Richard Beard was sent to the Forked Deer Circuit. Others soon followed, and in 1824 Hopewell Presbytery was ordered to be constituted at Bethel meetinghouse in Carroll County.

Other presbyteries organized during the period of the first

synod included Barnett (1827), St. Louis (1828), Princeton (1828), and Sangamon (1828).

As early as 1818 missionaries had been sent to the Chickasaw and Choctaw Indians in Mississippi and Alabama. In the fall of 1820, a school known as Charity Hall was established under the leadership of Robert Bell at a point near the present site of Aberdeen, Mississippi. The school continued to operate until 1832 when it was closed because of unrest occasioned by plans for the removal of the Indians to the West.

Within nineteen years after the organization of its first presbytery, the Cumberland Presbyterian Church had effectively reached into eight states and territories: Tennessee, Kentucky, Indiana, Illinois, Missouri, Arkansas, Alabama, and Mississippi.

FROM THE FORMATION OF THE GENERAL ASSEMBLY TO THE WAR BETWEEN THE STATES

Cumberland Synod, in 1828, resolved to form a General Assembly and made provision for the formation of four synods: Missouri, to consist of the presbyteries of McGee, Barnett, Sangamon, Illinois, St. Louis, and Arkansas; Green River, to consist of the presbyteries of Anderson, Princeton, Logan, and Indiana; Franklin, to consist of the presbyteries of Nashville, Lebanon, Knoxville, and Hopewell; and Columbia, to consist of the presbyteries of Alabama (which had been reorganized in 1824), Bigby, Elk, and Tennessee.

The third General Assembly, in 1831, sent Robert Donnell, Alexander Chapman, Reuben Burrow, John Morgan, and Alfred M. Bryan as missionaries to the East. This action was taken in response to a letter received from some Presbyterians in western Pennsylvania who had heard of the Cumberland Presbyterian Church and its doctrines and had invited the General Assembly to send ministers to that area. Some of these ministers remained in Pennsylvania, and Pennsylvania Presbytery, which first appears on the records of the General Assembly in 1833, was organized. One Presbyterian minister, the Reverend Jacob Lindley, and his congregation came over to the Cumberland Presbyterians. This area was made the setting for Dr. J. B. Logan's story, *Alice McDonald*.

In 1832 three new synods were created: Mississippi, consisting of the presbyteries of Alabama, Mississippi, and Elyton; Illinois, consisting of the presbyteries of Illinois, Sangamon, St. Louis, and Vandalia; and Western District (later West Tennessee) consisting of the presbyteries of Hopewell, Forked-Deer, and Hatchie. The latter synod included the portions of Tennessee and Kentucky lying west of the Tennessee River. A fourth presbytery, Obion, was created by this synod at its first meeting.

The pioneer Cumberland Presbyterian minister in Texas was Sumner Bacon, a New Englander who had joined the Cumberland Presbyterian Church in northwestern Arkansas but had been denied admittance to Arkansas Presbytery, reportedly because of his buckskin clothing and the peculiar nature of his call. (He claimed that his call was to preach only in Texas.) Bacon is known to have been in Texas as early as 1830, but it was not until the organization of Louisiana Presbytery at Alexandria, Louisiana, in 1835, that he was received under the care of a presbytery. Here he was received as a candidate, licensed, and ordained, all at the same meeting. In 1837 Texas Presbytery was organized by Sumner Bacon, Amos Roark, and Mitchell Smith. Both Louisiana and Texas Presbyteries were connected with the Synod of Mississippi. Louisiana Presbytery functioned mainly in southern Louisiana in the vicinity of Alexandria and Opelousas and was short-lived.

The church in Ohio was an extension of the church in Pennsylvania. Jacob Lindley had previously served as pastor of Presbyterian churches in eastern Ohio, and in company with John Morgan held a camp meeting near Athens, Ohio, in 1832. The newly formed churches in Ohio were supplied for several years by ministers from Pennsylvania. Some of these were churches which withdrew from the Presbyterian Church to become Cumberland Presbyterian congregations. Athens Presbytery, the first presbytery of the Cumberland Presbyterian Church in Ohio, first appears on the records of the General Assembly in 1837.

Meanwhile, Cumberland Presbyterians were following the

advancing frontier into the Northwest. David Lowry undertook
a mission to the Winnebago Indians. He organized the first Cumberland Presbyterian church in Iowa. It was composed of soldiers,
officers of the United States army, government employees, and a
few Indians. In 1844 Iowa Presbytery was organized.

A Cumberland Presbyterian minister, the Reverend J. A.
Cornwall, arrived in Oregon at the head of a group of colonists in
1846, the year in which the boundary of Oregon was settled by
treaty. The Reverend J. E. Braly and his family went in 1847.
Other ministers followed, and in 1851 the Oregon Presbytery
was organized. Four congregations were represented in the first
meeting.

The first Cumberland Presbyterian minister in California was
the above mentioned John E. Braly, who began his ministry there
in 1849, the year of the gold rush. The Reverend T. A. Ish and
the Reverend Cornelius Yager arrived in 1850. On April 4,
1851, the California Presbytery was organized without an order
from any synod. The General Assembly was asked to recognize
the new presbytery and attach it to some synod. The request
was granted, and the presbytery was attached to the Synod of
Missouri, which also included Oregon Presbytery.

As early as 1855, the year after Kansas was opened to white
settlers, the first Cumberland Presbyterian church in Kansas was
organized by the Reverend C. B. Hodges. In November of the
same year Kansas Presbytery was organized.

During the latter part of this period, attention was increasingly given to organizing churches in the cities. In earlier years
Cumberland Presbyterians had taken the gospel mostly to remote
frontier settlements. Cities began to spring up, however, in the
territories already occupied, and the need for a strategy for
establishing churches in the cities became apparent. The work
was difficult, however, for Cumberland Presbyterians had not
been educated to give liberally of their means.

The first board of missions for the entire church was organized in 1845. By 1860 twenty urban missions had been undertaken. These included Burlington, Iowa; Louisville and Paducah,

Kentucky; Cincinnati, Ohio; Philadelphia, Pennsylvania; Evansville, Indiana; St. Louis, Missouri; Alton and Peoria, Illinois; Leavenworth, Kansas; Mobile, Alabama; Clarksville, Murfreesboro, Jackson, Shelbyville, and Memphis, Tennessee; and Austin, Jefferson, and San Antonio, Texas.

The first missionary work by Cumberland Presbyterians among the Indians after their removal to Oklahoma was done by ministers from Red River Presbytery, in northeast Texas. The first Cumberland Presbyterian congregation in the Choctaw nation was organized in 1848 by the Reverend W. A. Provine. Others who did missionary work among the Indians in southeastern Oklahoma included the Reverend W. R. Baker, the Reverend Samuel Corley, and the Reverend David Lowry. In 1860, by order of Texas Synod, Bethel Presbytery was organized. It consisted of three Indian ministers—Israel Folsom and George Folsom, who were Choctaws, and Dixon Frazier, a Chickasaw; and three white ministers—W. R. Baker, Alexander Campbell, and R. S. Bell.

By 1860, in addition to the eight states which had been occupied prior to the organization of the General Assembly, the Cumberland Presbyterian Church had planted churches in Pennsylvania, Ohio, Louisiana, Texas, Iowa, Oregon, California, Kansas, and the Indian Territory (later Oklahoma).

FROM THE WAR BETWEEN THE STATES TO 1910

Just before the War Between the States, beginnings had been made toward planting churches in north Louisiana. Ministers from Marshall Presbytery, in Texas, had organized churches at Grand Cane and New Bethany, and ministers from Ouachita Presbytery, in southern Arkansas, had crossed the state line and organized several churches, among them one at Arcadia which was later moved out to its present location known as Oak Grove. In 1872 a new Louisiana Presbytery was organized with S. S. Smart, Joslin Jones, and G. N. Clampitt as ministers. It was organized by order of Ouachita Synod.

The first Cumberland Presbyterian church in Nebraska territory was organized on July 16, 1865, at Nebraska City, by the Reverend C. B. Hodges. Other churches were soon organized, and in 1873 Nebraska Presbytery was organized.

In November, 1870, three ministers—B. F. Moore, J. Cal Littrell, and S. D. Givens—participated in the organization of Rocky Mountain Presbytery, in the territory of Colorado. There was only one congregation under the care of this presbytery at the beginning, but by 1872 there were six.

In 1872, the Reverend H. E. Eagan migrated to the newly organized Washington territory and began preaching in the town of Walla Walla. A church was soon organized there. In 1874 or 1875 Cascade Presbytery was organized. Shortly afterward its name was changed to Walla Walla Presbytery.

Small beginnings were made during this period in West Virginia and New Jersey by extension from the churches in Pennsylvania. Other work was begun in Georgia, through migration from East Tennessee and eastern Alabama, and in Florida.

During the War Between the States, aid to city missions largely ceased except for some aid given by the board at Alton, Illinois, to mission points in Illinois, Kansas, and Iowa, and aid given by the Board of Pacific Synod to missions at Stockton and San Francisco, California. Between 1870 and 1905, however, at least seventy-seven urban mission churches were attempted.[3] Of these churches, fifty-four had become self-sustaining by the end of the period.

In addition to the work which was already in progress among the Chickasaw and Choctaw Indians, work among the Cherokees was begun in northeastern Oklahoma in about 1876. The first missionary there was the Reverend N. J. Crawford. In February, 1884, Cherokee Presbytery was organized with three ministers participating: the Reverend N. J. Crawford, the Reverend David Hogan, and the Reverend R. C. Parks. Its organization was ordered by Arkansas Synod.

As white settlers began to pour into Oklahoma and the Indian Territory, Cumberland Presbyterian churches were organized among them. Some of these represented a westward extension from King Presbytery, in western Arkansas, and eventually formed South McAlister Presbytery. Others represented a northward extension of Guthrie Presbytery, in north Texas. In that area Chickasaw Presbytery was organized in 1890. A third area to be evangelized was Greer County, then supposed to be a part of Texas. Greer County Presbytery was organized in 1891. Finally, there was a southward extension from Wichita Presbytery, in Kansas, which resulted in the organization of some five churches in northern Oklahoma. In 1900 these churches became a part of the new Oklahoma Presbytery.

There was, of course, further expansion as the frontiers advanced across some of the states mentioned earlier. In many instances the Cumberland Presbyterian Church was the first church organized in the community. An example of this sort of expansion is to be found in the new towns built along the Fort Worth and Denver Railroad in the late 1880's. As early as 1887, Gregory Presbytery, then the westernmost presbytery in north Texas, took note of the vast areas which were opening up and appointed the Reverend J. A. Zinn, the Reverend G. P. Hester, and the Reverend Thomas C. Bigham as missionaries to that area. At the fall meeting the Reverend J. A. Zinn reported having organized two churches. In May, 1889, four churches were received under the care of Gregory Presbytery, three of them being in the western part of the presbytery, namely, Chillicothe, Seymour, and Vernon. In April, 1890, seven churches were received under the care of the presbytery. These included Quanah, Harrold, and Childress. Another was Head Quarters, in Greer County. At this meeting of presbytery a petition was addressed to Texas Synod asking that a new presbytery to be known as Pease River Presbytery be created. By the spring of 1891, there were twenty-five organized churches in Pease River Presbytery. Ten of these had been under the care of Gregory Presbytery. Presumably the remainder had been organized within the year. In the fall of 1891, Pease River Presbytery was divided to form Greer County Presbytery.

The march of the Cumberland Presbyterian Church along the advancing frontier was brought to an abrupt halt as a result of the losses sustained in the attempted union with the Presbyterian Church, U.S.A., in 1906 (see chapter 10). In most areas a struggle for existence necessarily occupied the attention of the remaining ministers and their scattered flocks.

There was, however, at least one exception. About that time the Santa Fe Railroad was crossing the South Plains of Texas from north to south. As a result of a plan formulated at a meeting of Sweetwater Presbytery, which was also attended by ministers from Amarillo Presbytery, four evangelistic teams composed of two ministers each were sent out to strategic points immediately following the adjournment of presbytery. One result of this effort was the organization in August, 1908, of a church in Lubbock with seven members. With Lubbock as a hub, other small congregations already in existence, or soon afterward organized, constituted a sort of circuit to which the first pastor of the Lubbock church, the Reverend J. L. Elliott, ministered. Lubbock, now a city of more than 125,000 people, still forms the hub of the present Western Presbytery of Texas Synod.

In 1910, a small congregation was reported at Floyd, New Mexico. In 1912, Texas Synod ordered the organization of Roswell Presbytery. Perhaps half a dozen small congregations are listed as belonging to this presbytery during the next few years. One of these was near Pecos, Texas, the others in New Mexico. The coming of World War I and two years of severe drouth broke up this small presbytery, and all its congregations disappeared.

During the period from 1860 to 1910, the Cumberland Presbyterian Church planted churches in Nebraska, Colorado, Washington, Georgia, Florida, West Virginia, New Jersey, New Mexico, and Oklahoma. During the first century of its existence, the Cumberland Presbyterian Church had preached the gospel to four tribes of Indians and had planted churches in twenty-five states.

SOMETHING TO THINK ABOUT

1. What does the extent of the missionary work done by the "Council" indicate as to the evangelistic zeal of those who constituted the council?

2. How can we account for the rapid expansion of the Cumberland Presbyterian Church during its earlier years?

3. What did the work of a circuit rider involve? How would you evaluate the work of the circuit riders in the growth of the new church?

4. Why were Cumberland Presbyterians slow about establishing churches in the cities?

5. Through what channels was the gospel first brought to your community?

6. When was your local church organized, and by whom? Has a history of your church been written?

6. Negro Cumberland Presbyterians

NEGRO SLAVERY IN the western hemisphere had its beginning in 1562 when Sir John Hawkins, a famous English captain, secured a cargo of slaves on the west coast of Africa and sold them in the Spanish colonies in the West Indies. About a century later the slave trade began in earnest. The leaders in this enterprise were New England traders who exchanged rum for slaves. For a time slaves were to be found in every New England colony, but by the time of the War for Independence slavery had become largely a southern institution.

The Cumberland Presbyterian Church had its beginning in a state where slavery existed. Of the sixteen states into which the Cumberland Presbyterian Church had penetrated prior to 1860, eight were slave states; however, the membership of the Cumberland Presbyterian Church was far larger in these eight states than in the eight where slavery was prohibited.

ATTITUDES TOWARD SLAVERY

Two of the three ministers who constituted the Cumberland Presbytery in 1810 are known to have opposed slavery. McAdow moved from Tennessee to Illinois some ten years after the organization of the new presbytery. One reason for his moving was said to be the fact that he did not wish his children to become involved in the institution of slavery.[1] Finis Ewing, the only one of the three who ever owned slaves, gave his slaves their freedom. His concern over the institution of slavery is expressed in the following excerpt from a published sermon of his on "The Duty of the Church":

> "But, where shall we begin? O! is it indeed true that in this enlightened age, there are so many palpable evils in the church that it is difficult to know where to commence enumerating them? The first evil which I will mention is a *traffic in human flesh and human souls!* It is true, that many professors of religion, and I fear some of my Cumberland brethren, do not scruple to *sell for life* their fellow beings, some of whom are their brethren in the Lord. And what is worse, they are not scrupulous to whom they sell, provided they can obtain a better price! Sometimes husbands and wives, parents and children are thus separated, and I doubt not their cries reach the ears of the Lord of Sabaoth.
>
> "(Lest some of my readers should say, 'physician heal thyself,' I think it proper to state in this place, that after a *long, painful,* and prayerful investigation of this subject, I have determined *not* to *hold,* nor to *give,* nor to *sell,* nor to *buy any slave for life.* Mainly from the influence of that passage of God's word which says, 'Masters give unto your servants that which is *just* and *equal.*')
>
> "Others who constitute a part of the visible church *half*-feed, *half*-clothe, and *oppress* their servants. Indeed, they seem by their conduct towards them *not* to consider them *fellow-beings.* And it is to be feared that many of them are taking no pains at all to give their servants religious instruction of any kind, and especially are they making no efforts to teach them or cause them to be taught to read that book which testifies of Jesus. While others permit, perhaps require their servants to work, cook, &c., while the white people are praying around the family altar." [2]

McDonnold quotes several anti-slavery editorials from *The Revivalist* and *The Cumberland Presbyterian* published during the period from 1830 to 1836. McDonnold further states that he never knew an extreme pro-slavery man among the members of the Cumberland Presbyterian Church. That a number of Cumberland Presbyterians owned slaves is undoubtedly true, although the number of Cumberland Presbyterians who were of the landed aristocracy and had any considerable vested interest in the institution of slavery was probably small.

When the question of slavery became more acutely a sectional and political issue, there was a reaction among Cumberland Presbyterians in the South, as among other southern people, against abolitionism. Thus when Pennsylvania Synod passed a resolution in 1847 stating "That the system of slavery in the United States is contrary to the principles of the gospel, hinders the progress thereof, and ought to be abolished," notice of this action was taken by the committee of the next General Assembly which reviewed these minutes. The report of this committee, which was concurred in by the Assembly, expressed disapproval of the synod's action and the fear that such resolutions, if persisted in, would tend to produce strife.[3]

Athens Presbytery, which was situated in Ohio, passed a resolution in the summer of 1848 recommending that its church sessions not grant the sacramental privileges and immunities to any person who justified slavery as practiced in the United States. At least one southern presbytery adopted a resolution suggesting that the proceedings of Athens Presbytery violated the Constitution of the church and "ought to be revoked by the proper authorities as speedily as possible and that the peace of the church demand it." [4]

Among Cumberland Presbyterians the only abolitionist sentiment appearing in the official records during this period seems to have come out of Ohio and Pennsylvania. It has been noted that many Cumberland Presbyterians in Illinois, Iowa, California, and the Northwest had migrated from the South and probably tended to think more like southern people.[5] In any case the prevailing sentiment in the General Assembly at this time seemed to be that the church should not become involved in what were regarded by some as sectional and political issues. Consequently, all legislation on the subject of slavery was discouraged.

After the war, most Cumberland Presbyterians were glad slavery had been abolished. McDonnold, writing in the 1880's, says,

> "As to the present attitude of our people in regard to the now old and thrice-dead slavery issue, the writer does

not know a Cumberland Presbyterian of any section who is not heartily glad that the negro is free." [6]

NEGROES IN THE CHURCH DURING THE PRE-WAR PERIOD

It is not known just when or where Cumberland Presbyterians first became concerned about the evangelization of Negro slaves. But it must have been quite early in the history of the denomination, for McDonnold states that before the war there were twenty thousand Negro Cumberland Presbyterians. He states that Negro members attended the same services with the white people, although separate seats were provided.[7] Some church buildings with balconies that were originally built to accommodate slaves still stand.[8]

The Negroes had preachers of their own race who held special services for them in addition to the services in which both races participated. At such services, the laws of most states required the presence of a responsible white man. Negro ministers were licensed and ordained by the same presbyteries in which the white ministers held membership. It was necessary to make some exceptions in the educational requirements. How many Negro ministers there were in the Cumberland Presbyterian Church, we have no way of knowing. Edmond Weir, a Negro and the first foreign missionary sent out by the Cumberland Presbyterian Church, is said to have been ordained by Anderson Presbytery. That there were others is indicated by the fact that an effort was made to induce Cumberland Presbyterians who owned ordained ministers to release them so that they might join Weir in Liberia.

The following quotation from the session record of a church which had some ten or twelve Negro slaves as members prior to the close of the War Between the States illustrates the usual practice followed in recording their admission:

> "Servant George (Spence) Andrew (Love) and Bob (Shelton) were received by letter from M E Church South as members of Corsicana congregation. Servant Rachel (Spence) was received by recommendation as a member of Corsicana congregation." [9]

As early as 1838 a Negro slave presented himself to Texas Presbytery.

> "Charles Polk's colored man, Tennessee, petitioned the Pres. for leave to exercise his gift in reading the Scriptures, singing, prayer and exhortation among his colored friends, and having produced testimonials of his good moral conduct; of his communion in the church; and the Pres. having examined him as to his experimental acquaintance with Religion; as to his internal impressions and the motives which induced him to desire this liberty—With Mr. Polk's consent, his petition was granted." [10]

THE CHANGED RELATIONSHIP AFTER THE WAR

With the close of the war and the emancipation of the slaves in the South, relationships between the races were changed. The northern churches had begun missionary work in the South during the war, and they continued their efforts during the period of reconstruction. The southern churches also recognized their obligation to the ex-slaves and worked toward forming them into separate churches. A Special Committee on the Moral and Religious Training of the Colored People, appointed by the General Assembly in 1866, expressed the opinion (which did not go unchallenged) "that no class of citizens are so well prepared, nor are those any more willing to aid them, than those with whom this people have always lived." The report of this committee, which was concurred in by the General Assembly, contained the following recommendations:

> "1. That the General Assembly recommend that all the Presbyteries of the church, take such steps as may be most expedient to organize for them Sabbath schools, and supply them with suitable books and teachers.
> "2. That they co-operate with the American Bible Society in supplying them with the Word of God.
> "3. That they use every means, so far as they can, to afford them the means of grace and encourage them to sustain the same, as God may prosper them.
> "4. That they aid them so far as they can, in obtaining houses suitable for such schools and the more public worship of God." [11]

The report of the committee on missions the following year contained equally strong recommendations for the evangelization and religious instruction of the Negro people. Even in the recommendations adopted in 1866, however, there are intimations that segregated churches and sabbath schools were contemplated.

One southern presbytery in the fall of 1867 reported "about six hundred conversions among whites, and two hundred and fifty coloreds converted." It was further reported that "There were about four hundred 'accessions' among whites and about one hundred among the coloreds." One Negro licentiate is listed.[12] Thus far it would appear that work among the Negroes was continuing as in former years. This presbytery, however, was directed by synod to define the ecclesiastical status of this Negro licentiate, and presbytery in its spring meeting in 1868 reported "that it is the sense of this Presbytery that his licensure does not convey with nor was it intended to give him the right or privilege to labor with any only those of his own color." [13]

In July, 1866, another presbytery in the South had officially recognized in the Negro population "a field for moral & mental improvement already white unto the harvest" but suggested that the Negro should be instructed "by persons whose interests & associations are identical with ours." [14] The same presbytery, in a meeting held in December, 1867, recognizing that it did not have the laborers to cultivate the field presented by the colored population, resolved to license "worthy colored men to preach to their Brethren, perform the rites of matrimony, and the ordinances of baptism, when in our judgment they may be qualified for such work." The resolution hastened to add, however, that "nothing in the foregoing shall be construed as entitling them to seats in any of the judicatures of our church." [15] Thus the pattern of segregation was fast developing. The Negroes seemed to want their own separate churches, and the white people were glad this was so.

Dr. William Warren Sweet, commenting on the situation in this period, writes, "The Negroes were now free and many of them, if for no other reason than to put their freedom to the test, were anxious to separate themselves from the churches of their former masters. In many cases the Negroes were suspicious of the intention of the southern churches, in which they had formerly worshiped under the eye of their white masters, with the result that the

Negro membership of the old southern churches rapidly decreased." [16]

A NEGRO CUMBERLAND PRESBYTERIAN CHURCH IS CREATED

Such was the situation when in 1869 the General Assembly met in Murfreesboro, Tennessee. A convention of Negro Cumberland Presbyterians was called for the same time to meet in the same city. This convention formulated resolutions asking the General Assembly to authorize the creation of separate presbyteries of colored ministers and to make provision for the organization of a synod as soon as the requisite number of presbyteries could be formed. The church was also asked to co-operate by lending them church houses, aiding them in building church houses of their own, providing them with books, and making provision whereby the colored ministers might be instructed in theology and church government. The Colored Convention expressed the opinion "that it would not be for the advancement of the Church, among either the white or colored race, for the ministers of the two races to meet together in the same judicatures." With this opinion the General Assembly concurred.[17] Thus, at their own request, provision was made for the Negro constituency to be formed into a separate church, a fact of which they were later reminded more than once. (A similar situation developed in the Methodist Episcopal Church, South, for in 1870 the Colored Methodist Episcopal Church was constituted out of Negro members of the southern branch of Methodism.)

At the General Assembly in 1871, it was noted that three presbyteries of Negroes had been organized: Greenville Presbytery, within the bounds of the Synod of Green River, and Huntsville and Elk River Presbyteries, in the bounds of the Synod of Columbia. They requested that they be organized into a synod. The General Assembly therefore directed the organization of a synod to be known as the First Synod of the Colored Cumberland Presbyterian Church. Its first meeting was to be held at Fayetteville, Tennessee, on Friday before the first Sabbath of November, 1871.[18] In 1874, a General Assembly was organized. That year the corresponding delegate to the white General Assembly reported that the Colored Cumberland Presbyterian Church had forty-six ordained ministers, twenty licentiates, thirty candidates for the ministry, and three thousand communicants. McDonnold states that only a very small portion of the twenty thousand Negroes who were in the Cumberland Presbyterian Church prior to 1860 were ever brought into the new church. By 1886, however, the membership of the Negro denomination had grown to about fifteen thousand.

RELATIONS BETWEEN THE TWO CHURCHES, 1869-1937

In 1870, the year following the decision to set up a separate church for the Negroes, the Reverend Moses T. Weir, a brother of the missionary to Liberia, appeared with a commission from Greenville Presbytery asking for a seat in the General Assembly. An adverse decision was given on the ground that there was no proper information before the Assembly concerning the organization or existence of Greenville Presbytery.[19] In 1873, there was a memorial from nine ministers and elders of Missouri Presbytery asking the General Assembly to decide whether they were members of Ozark Synod (a white synod in Missouri) or of a colored synod in Kentucky or Tennessee and whether they were entitled to representation in the General Assembly. The General Assembly cited the action of 1869, emphasizing that the Negroes had "chosen their own status." [20] Such decisions were made solely on the basis of the actions taken in 1869. Actually, there is nothing in the Constitution of the Cumberland Presbyterian Church which would make race a bar to membership. There was at least one Negro congregation in the Cumberland Presbyterian Church from about 1899 until 1906.[21] Of course, this was the exception rather than the rule.

One of the requests made by the convention at Murfreesboro in 1869 was that some plan be presented by which Negro ministers might receive instruction in theology and church government. By 1885 there was a school of the Colored Cumberland Presbyterian Church at Bowling Green, Kentucky. A proposal was made to the General Assembly of the Cumberland Presbyterian Church that the Reverend M. M. Smith (then pastor of the white church in Bowling Green) be employed to teach theology in this school. The committee to which the proposal was referred, however, hesitated "to recommend anything that might embarrass the General Assembly financially." Sometime prior to 1897 the school at Bowling Green was sold. Then there was an unsuccessful effort to establish a school at Springfield, Missouri.

In 1898 the General Assembly advised the General Assembly of the Cumberland Presbyterian Church, Colored, to arrange for its probationers to attend Fisk University, at Nashville, until such time as a college could be established by the church. In 1899 and 1900 there were requests for nominal financial support for schools of the Negro church located at Huntsville, Alabama, and Newbern, Tennessee, but no positive action was taken by the white Assembly.

The Cumberland Presbyterian Church, Colored, was not directly involved in the attempted union of the Cumberland Presbyterian Church with the Presbyterian Church, U. S. A., in 1903-1906. After the attempted union, the Cumberland Presbyterian Church found itself so involved in its own problems that even less assistance was given the Negro church than before. Only occasionally was a voice raised in favor of doing something to aid the Cumberland Presbyterian Church, Colored. One such voice was that of the Reverend J. L. Hudgins, who in 1926 wrote an article which appeared in *The Cumberland Presbyterian,* which he edited. Among other things he said:

> "We are in full sympathy with our one thousand Cumberland Presbyterians in China, and are expressing our sympathy in a substantial way, but why should we, as far as any organized efforts are concerned, fail to show our sympathy for something like 15,000 Cumberland Presbyterians in our homeland because their skin is not of the same hue as our own? We believe the Cumberland Presbyterian Church should give as many dollars every year to help our brethren in black as it gives to help our brethren in yellow, and we would see the Cumberland Presbyterian Church, Colored, growing and progressing." [22]

CO-OPERATIVE EFFORTS SINCE 1937

In 1937, at the General Assembly held at Knoxville, Tennessee, a resolution introduced by the Reverend E. K. Reagin was adopted with reference to the Cumberland Presbyterian Church, Colored. It pointed out that "this church is now in serious need of help in the form of personal direction in the solution of their problems." The Board of Missions and Church Erection was directed to create within the board a committee to study the conditions and needs of this church, offer assistance to the leaders of the church in the church courts and programs of their boards, and to make further recommendations to the Assembly. The next General Assembly provided for a continuation of this sort of co-operation and adopted the further recommendation "That each Presbytery study the needs of the Colored Cumberland Presbyterian Churches within its bounds, give the needed assistance if possible, and report to this committee its findings."

From 1944 through 1947, the youth groups of the Cumberland Presbyterian Church contributed to the erection of a church building for Cumberland Presbyterian Negroes in Muskogee, Oklahoma. Beginning with an institute held at Jacksonville, Texas, in 1949, synodic institutes for adults and young people of the Colored Cumberland Presbyterian Church were sponsored, first by the Board of Christian Education and subsequently by the Board of Missions and Evangelism and the Board of Publication and Christian Education jointly. Beginning in 1951, a youth camp sponsored by Texas Synod was held each year for several years at Jarvis Christian College, Hawkins, Texas. Offerings taken in vacation church schools of the Cumberland Presbyterian Church were used to provide workers to conduct demonstration vacation church schools in various areas of the Negro Cumberland Presbyterian Church and to provide funds for purchase of a lot for Negro Cumberland Presbyterians in Dallas, Texas. During the year 1952, Cumberland Youth Fellowships provided funds with which Mr. E. L. Wallace, a Negro layman, was employed for ten weeks to do special promotional work among the Negro Cumberland Presbyterian churches.

In 1948, a commission was appointed "to study the needs of the Negro Cumberland Presbyterian Church and make a written report to the next General Assembly with recommendations as to any assistance, co-operation, and financial aid which we might be able to give the Negro Church to further their cause and strengthen them as a denomination among their people." There is no report on record of the commission as such, but the report of the Board of Missions and Church Erection in 1949 and the reports of the Board of Missions and Evangelism for subsequent years recognized Negro missions as one phase of the work of the Board. Since 1957, the Board of Missions and Evangelism has helped promote a camp each year for Negro Cumberland Presbyterian young people. This camp is held at the camp site owned by Kentucky Synod near Morgantown, Kentucky.

Some assistance has been given the Negro church through boards of missions of some of the presbyteries of the Cumberland Presbyterian Church. For example, Madison Presbytery, through its board of missions, is contributing $600 annually to aid the Mt. Tabor church, near Jackson, Tennessee, the only Negro Cumberland Presbyterian church within its bounds.

In 1950, provision was made for the exchange of fraternal delegates by the General Assemblies of the two churches. Fraternal delegates were exchanged for the first time in 1951. Under this provision each synod is asked to appoint a fraternal delegate to the General Assembly of the other church. In 1957, the General Assembly adopted a recommendation that a similar exchange of fraternal delegates be promoted on the synodical and presbyterial levels. This recommendation has been carried out only in part.

During 1950, Cumberland Youth Fellowship groups contributed to a fund for scholarships to aid in the education of Negro ministerial students. A similar project was promoted again in 1958. In 1953, by action of the General Assembly, a memorial from Texas Synod asking for the admission of "Colored Cumberland Presbyterian Ministerial Candidates and other full time Christian workers" to the Cumberland Presbyterian Theological Seminary was granted. One Negro student enrolled in the Seminary in the fall of 1956 but had to withdraw because of ill health. Very few ministerial candidates in the Negro Cumberland Presbyterian Church held a college degree, which is a prerequisite for entrance to the seminary. Some means of furthering the education of Negro ministers at a lower level was needed. In 1954, the General Assembly voted to open the In-Service Training School for Rural Ministers to Negro Cumberland Presbyterian ministers. The first Negro ministers attended the In-Service School in 1956. The General Assembly in 1959 had before it a memorial from the Synod of Oklahoma asking the Assembly "to instruct the Board of Trustees of Bethel College to at least admit qualified ministerial candidates to said college irrespective of the candidate's race or color." The General Assembly instructed the Board of Trustees of Bethel College "to study, prepare and propose a plan to the next General Assembly to implement a program which would comply with the spirit and objectives of this memorial." Two more Assemblies passed, however, before the Board of Trustees voted to admit qualified ministerial students of the Second Cumberland Presbyterian Church.[23] In the fall of 1961, one Negro ministerial student enrolled in Bethel College. In 1962-1963 there were two Negro students enrolled, and in 1963-1964, four Negro students. In 1964, the General Assembly directed that both Bethel College and the Theological Seminary be opened to all qualified students. One Negro Cumberland Presbyterian student entered Memphis Theological Seminary in the fall of 1964, and it is significant that he was a graduate of Bethel College.

The Second Cumberland Presbyterian Church has suffered from a shortage of competent ministerial leadership. Opening of the educational institutions of the Cumberland Presbyterian Church to its Negro brethren should in time help to alleviate this shortage. Despite the limitations of its resources, the Second Church has planted churches in such cities as Detroit, Michigan; Cleveland, Ohio; and Chicago, Illinois. It now consists of four synods and sixteen presbyteries and has churches in eleven states: Alabama, Tennessee, Kentucky, Illinois, Indiana, Ohio, Michigan, Iowa, Missouri, Oklahoma, and Texas. A monthly paper, *The Cumberland Flag,* is published at Union City, Tennessee.

EFFORTS TOWARD REUNION

In 1883, the General Assembly of the Cumberland Presbyterian Church had before it a memorial from the Synod of Central

Illinois asking that steps be taken to open the way for the restoration of the people of the Cumberland Presbyterian Church, Colored, to the Cumberland Presbyterian Church. This memorial was answered by the reminder that it was the Negroes themselves who chose to set up a separate church.

In 1957, Cherokee Presbytery, in northeastern Oklahoma, addressed a memorial to the General Assembly asking that a special committee be appointed to work with a similar committee from the Cumberland Presbyterian Church, Colored, "to study the feasibility of organic union between the two Cumberland Presbyterian denominations and to make recommendations to their respective General Assemblies in 1959 of the advisability of such a union." Provision was made for a committee, but it was composed of the moderator of the General Assembly and one member to be appointed from each board of the Assembly. The committees from the two churches reached an agreement that union was impractical at that time but that the possibiliy of such a union should not be abandoned. More co-operation on the presbyterial level was urged.

In 1959, the General Assembly of the Cumberland Presbyterian Church suggested to its committee that it work toward the goal of forming the Negro churches into one synod, and that this synod become a synod of the Cumberland Presbyterian Church. The Joint Committee of the two churches, after conference, reported that the proposal of the 1959 Assembly was not feasible.

These proposals originated within the white church and seemed to result in little progress toward a reunion of the two churches. In 1963, however, the General Assembly of the Second Cumberland Presbyterian Church took the initiative by inviting the Cumberland Presbyterian Church "to begin a discussion and set up machinery for initial talks on merger." A committee of seven from each church, with alternates, was named, and this joint committee held its first meeting in November, 1963. The joint committee, recognizing the need for a better knowledge on the part of each church of the constituency and program of the other, took steps to have studies made to achieve this end. It also adopted a theological basis for reunification, in which attention was centered on the demands of the Christian faith for the realization of a fellowship in love. The theological basis and the proposals for the studies designed to help the two churches to come to know each other better were approved by the general assemblies of both churches in 1964.

One of the most urgent needs is the establishment of better lines of communication between the two churches on the presbyterial and local levels in those areas where churches of both denominations exist. The recognition of what these two churches have in common, since both hold to the same Confession of Faith and form of government, would seem to be the place where ecumenical concerns should begin.

SOMETHING TO THINK ABOUT

1. What was the attitude of the founders and early leaders of the Cumberland Presbyterian Church toward slavery?

2. Why was there a tendency to discourage the passing of deliverances concerning slavery in the period immediately preceding the War Between the States? Is the attempt to confine the deliberations of the church to so-called "spiritual" matters ever an adequate answer?

3. What evidence is there that many Cumberland Presbyterians prior to the war were concerned about the spiritual welfare of the Negroes?

4. What circumstances in the period just after the war led to the formation of Negro churches?

5. How do you account for the meager support given the Negro Cumberland Presbyterian Church by the white church during most of its history? Is this consistent with the interest the white church has manifested in missions to people of other races and nationalities?

6. What efforts have been made to work with the Negro Cumberland Presbyterian Church since 1937? To what extent have these efforts been effective?

7. Is there a Negro Cumberland Presbyterian church near you? If so, what do you know concerning its activities? Would it be possible for an exchange of visits to be worked out?

7. In Regions Beyond

DURING THE FIRST forty years of its existence, the Cumberland Presbyterian Church concentrated its missionary efforts in frontier America. The General Assembly, however, did recommend co-operation with the American Board of Commissioners for Foreign Missions. This board had been formed in June, 1810, under Congregational auspices, but in 1812 became interdenominational. It is known that some Cumberland Presbyterians offered themselves to, and were sent out by, this board.

THE FIRST EFFORT—LIBERIA

Liberia, on the coast of West Africa, was promoted by the American Colonization Society as a home for liberated slaves. Many of these slaves were Cumberland Presbyterians. In 1851, the General Assembly approved a recommendation that Liberia be designated as a mission field. The Reverend Edmond Weir, a liberated slave and a minister who had been ordained by Anderson Presbytery, reached Liberia in 1852. For five years he served as sheriff and preached without salary. In 1857, he returned to the United States to raise funds for a church building. While here he was commissioned as a missionary. An appeal was made for the release of other Cumberland Presbyterian ministers who were slaves to go with Weir, but none was made available. In 1859, land on which to build a church was obtained at Cape Mount.

Soon after the beginning of the War Between the States,

the Board of Missions with headquarters at Lebanon, Tennessee, became unable to operate. The work in Liberia was turned over to the newly created board at Alton, Illinois, but only meager support was given. In 1867, Weir returned to the United States, appeared before the Board of Missions, and toured the churches briefly. He returned to Liberia in November. The General Assembly in 1868 recommended that the mission be suspended. Weir subsequently transferred to the Congregational Church.

ATTEMPTED MISSION TO THE MOHAMMEDANS

In 1859, the Reverend J. C. Armstrong, a graduate of the theological school at Cumberland University who had become interested in preaching to the Mohammedans, offered himself to the Board of Missions. At the General Assembly in 1860, he was consecrated as a missionary to Turkey. Armstrong, his wife, and an infant son sailed from New York on August 7, 1860. In September, they arrived at Constantinople, where Armstrong engaged in a study of the Turkish langauge. Shortly thereafter he received a call from Brouza, some eighty miles away, where twenty priests and several thousand members had broken away from the Greek Orthodox Church. Two Greek preachers wanted to join him in forming a presbytery, but before the proper authorization could be obtained the War Between the States began. Armstrong was from the South, but other American missionaries in Turkey were northern sympathizers who adopted the extreme views of Greely and Beecher. Consequently, these missionaries would not aid Armstrong. Cut off from support from his own mission board, he and his family were reduced almost to starvation, but help came through unexpected channels. Armstrong, during his brief stay in Turkey, spent some time translating documents of a group of Armenian Christians whose doctrines he found to be similar to those of the Cumberland Presbyterian Church.

In December, 1861, Armstrong became ill. In July, 1862, he left for America by way of Britain. He went to Canada where he remained and taught school. The General Assembly in 1867 ordered the payment of $630 which was due Armstrong. Thus ended the attempt to plant a mission in Turkey.

TRINIDAD AND VENEZUELA

In 1870, the Board of Missions decided to renew its mission efforts in other lands. Dr. N. H. McGhirk, a Cumberland Presbyterian from Missouri who lived on the island of Trinidad, invited the Board to consider Trinidad as a mission field. The population of the island included Hindus, Chinese, Negroes, Spaniards, Portuguese, French, English, and a few Americans. Trinidad was to be a stepping stone to Venezuela. Some assurances had been given of a grant of land consisting of eight hundred square miles for a mission in Venezuela. At that time there was no Protestant missionary in Venezuela.

The Reverend S. T. Anderson was appointed a missionary to Trinidad and Venezuela in November, 1873. Dr. McGhirk was appointed as a lay helper. Soon after arriving in Trinidad, Anderson became supply pastor for a Presbyterian mission church in San Fernando which was under the direction of the Free Church of Scotland. Lack of funds prevented the sending of additional workers. The time spent in supplying the Presbyterian mission church, although it helped him financially, detracted Anderson from the purpose for which he came to Trinidad. In 1876, the board recalled him. The church had relied too much on an expected gift of land and on Anderson's supply work rather than on the sacrificial giving of its own people.

SUCCESS IN JAPAN

The Cumberland Presbyterian Church experienced three failures in its attempts to engage in foreign mission work. Some voices were raised in opposition to any further attempt, but the growing missionary spirit of the church would not give up.

In 1872, the Reverend M. L. Gordon was sent to Japan as a missionary under the American Board. He was a graduate of Waynesburg College and a Cumberland Presbyterian, and Pennsylvania Synod assumed his salary. His going attracted the attention of Cumberland Presbyterians to Japan.

In 1876, two brothers, the Reverend J. B. Hail and the Reverend A. D. Hail, graduates of Waynesburg College, were accepted as missionary candidates. In January, 1877, J. B. Hail and his family sailed for Japan. A. D. Hail went the next year, his salary being paid by Pennsylvania Synod. Work was begun at Osaka in 1879. The first converts were baptized in September, 1880. In February, 1884, a church was organized at Osaka with sixty-four members. A presbytery was organized sometime between 1885 and 1887.

In 1888, the General Assembly granted permission for the mission to become a part of the Church of Christ in Japan. The apparent success of this union was subsequently used as an argument for the union which was attempted with the Presbyterian Church, U. S. A., in 1903-1906.

By 1903, twenty-one American missionaries were connected with the Cumberland Presbyterian mission in Japan. There were at that time seven organized churches and eleven chapels with a total membership of 815. By 1906, there were 1,132 members.

In 1906, as a result of the attempted union with the Presbyterian Church, U. S. A., the Japanese mission passed under the control of the larger Presbyterian body. Nonetheless, the work begun under the direction of the Cumberland Presbyterian Church has lived on. Recently, as indicated by a letter from the Reverend Thomas Forester, the ministry rendered by the Cumberland Presbyterian Church through its mission to Japan during those early years has been attested by persons still living who either directly or indirectly came under its influence.[1]

THE WOMAN'S BOARD ORGANIZED

As a direct result of the peculiar needs of the Japanese mission field, the Woman's Board of Missions was organized. Early in 1880, the Reverend W. J. Darby, pastor of the First Cumberland Presbyterian Church of Evansville, Indiana, received a letter from the Reverend A. D. Hail urging that steps be taken at the next General Assembly, which was to convene at Evansville in May, to enlist the women of the church more actively in the work of foreign missions. Since the Japanese women could not be reached at their homes by men, the missionaries felt the need for having Bible women to work among the women of Japan.

Dr. Darby presented the matter to the women of his congregation. After clearing the matter with the General Assembly's Board of Missions, the Woman's Foreign Missionary Society of the Evansville church sent out an invitation to the women of the Cumberland Presbyterian Church, urging them to send representatives to a convention to be held at the same time and place as the General Assembly for the purpose of forming a Woman's Board of Foreign Missions. About seventy-five women met in Evansville on May 25, 1880, and the Woman's Board of Foreign Missions was organized. Provision was made for an annual convention and for the organization of auxiliaries. The board was to be located at Evansville. The General Assembly approved this action by unanimous vote.

The object of the Woman's Board, as set forth in the constitution, was "to promote an interest among the Christian women of the Cumberland Presbyterian Church in behalf of Foreign Missions, and to work in cooperation with the General Assembly's Board of Missions in sending the Gospel to the heathen." Specifically, the Woman's Board proposed to send young women to the foreign mission field.

In 1890, the charter was amended to permit this board to engage in home missions, and the name changed to Woman's Board of Missions. The Woman's Board helped establish schools for the Chinese in San Francisco, Hanford, and Merced, California. A mountain mission school was established by this board at Barnard, North Carolina, and assistance was given to the work among the Choctaw Indians in the Indian Territory (now Oklahoma).

Changing circumstances, following the attempted union with the Presbyterian Church, U. S. A., were to cast the Woman's Board in a new role—that of promoting and directing the entire program of foreign missions of the Cumberland Presbyterian Church. In 1938, with a view to enlisting the men of the church more actively in the work of foreign missions, three men were elected to membership on the board, and subsequently the name was changed to the Board of Foreign Missions.

MISSION TO MEXICO

In 1886, the Reverend A. H. Whatley, a graduate of Cumberland University, was sent as a missionary to Mexico. After some fourteen months spent in study of the language, the people, and the field, Aguas Calientes, a city of thirty-five thousand inhabitants located in the state of the same name, was selected as the base of operation. Here a church was organized in 1889. A school known as the Griffin Industrial School for boys was established in 1898. Likewise a school for girls, Colegio Morales, in which Miss Mary Turner and Miss Kate Spencer taught, was begun. This mission passed from the control of the Cumberland Presbyterian Church in 1906.

BEGINNINGS IN CHINA

On September 27, 1897, the first Cumberland Presbyterian missionaries to China arrived at Shanghai. They were Dr. and Mrs. O. T. Logan, who went as medical missionaries. Chang-teh, in the province of Hunan in southeast central China, was chosen as the site for the mission. The missionaries reached Chang-teh on December 25, 1898. They were joined soon afterward by the Reverend T. J. Preston. In 1899, Dr. William Kelley was sent to assist in the work, his salary being paid by the Christian Endeavor societies of the church. Late in 1900, the mission had to be abandoned temporarily because of the Boxer Rebellion, but it was reopened in 1901. By 1906, there was a hospital at Chang-teh and churches had been organized at Chang-teh and Tao Yuen.

The work in Hunan province passed from the control of the Cumberland Presbyterian Church in 1906, but the work was continued under the direction of the Presbyterian Church, U. S. A., as were the missions in Japan and Mexico. Dr. Logan continued in this work until he met his death at the hand of an insane soldier whom he was attending on December 17, 1919. The Reverend T. J. Preston was still on the field in 1920.

THE STRANGER WITHIN OUR GATES

Many orientals came to the United States during the latter

part of the nineteenth century, the majority of them settling in California. A work was therefore begun in San Francisco, which not only proved to be a fruitful field in its own right but was to become a stepping stone by which again a Cumberland Presbyterian missionary would enter China.

In January, 1894, a mission school was opened. Mrs. J. J. Sitton taught English to young men and boys recently come from China. She also cared for sick Chinese children and adopted some of them. In 1898, a Sunday school was started, and the following year a night school was organized.

Meanwhile, a young man named Gam Sing Quah came from his native home in China to America, seeking material gain. In 1890 he was converted to Christianity in Fort Worth, Texas, under the ministry of Dr. R. M. Tinnon. From 1891 to 1900, he attended Cumberland University at Lebanon, Tennessee. On May 10, 1899, he was ordained to the full work of the ministry by Lebanon Presbytery.

He desired to return to China. It was concluded that he would not fit into the work in Hunan Province but, rather, that he should be sent as soon as possible to work among his own people in the vicinity of Canton. Meanwhile, he was assigned to work among the Chinese in San Francisco. He also worked at Hanford and Merced, serving as interpreter, preacher, and evangelist. In 1904, a church was organized among the Chinese in San Francisco. One of the two original elders was Tom Jung, who later succeeded Gam Sing Quah as pastor of the church.

In 1906, Gam Sing Quah was the only missionary who remained in the Cumberland Presbyterian Church. He was employed by the General Assembly's Board of Missions. The Woman's Board of Missions, after reorganization following the loss of all except two of its members, found itself in 1907 in the peculiar position of "being a Missionary Board without a missionary, and with no definite work in sight." It was immediately requested, however, to assume one-half the expense of the San Francisco Chinese Mission. In 1908, Gam Sing Quah informed the Woman's Board that he must return to China to work among his people there. This necessitated readjustments in the work at

San Francisco as well as provision for the expense of sending him to China. The work, however, was carried on.

In 1920, the Woman's Board resolved to provide new buildings for Canton and San Francisco. (Gam Sing Quah had returned to the United States that year for the first time since beginning his work in China.) Throughout the church the women sang "Build Two Missions in 1920." The new building in San Francisco became a reality. The Reverend D. W. Fooks, stated clerk of the General Assembly, was sent to direct the erection of the new building which was completed at a cost of $28,000.

In 1952, Dr. Samuel King Gam, son of Gam Sing Quah, succeeded the Reverend Tom Jung as pastor in San Francisco. He served until his untimely death in June, 1955. In November, 1955, Reverend Paul K. F. Wu became pastor. A new church building was completed in 1958. In 1960, the church had a Sunday school enrollment of 370 with a preponderance of children and young people. In addition to a full program of the usual church activities, there is a Chinese language school with an enrollment (in 1965) of 225 and an evening English language school for persons recently arrived from China.

In 1961, the mission became known officially as the Chinese Cumberland Presbyterian Church; however, the Board of Foreign Missions continues support of the Reverend and Mrs. Davis O. Bryson, who direct the youth work.

This church is said to have been the first church in Chinatown to have a party in the church building, the first to use choir robes, the first to have a movie projector, the first to have a neon sign, and the first to build a new sanctuary.

GAM RETURNS TO CHINA

It has already been noted that the Reverend Gam Sing Quah returned to China in 1908. Sending him seemed an impossible task due to the disrupted state of the church at that time, but his salary was provided first by Knoxville Presbytery and then for many years by Kentucky Synod.

Gam had difficulty in renting a house in which to begin his mission work. After having to move once, he succeeded in renting a house which no one else would have because it was believed to be haunted. Through street preaching, visitation, and personal work, he carried the gospel to the people. In February, 1911, a girls' school was opened. Churches at Canton and Sha Kai were organized in 1912. These were placed under the care of California Presbytery. In 1914, missions were begun at Honam and Ti Won, and in 1915 at Tai Chung. As a result of the above mentioned campaign for mission buildings, launched in 1920, a new building was erected in Canton and was dedicated June 15, 1922.

In 1924, a petition was sent by the Woman's Missionary Convention to the General Assembly asking that the Reverend D. W. Fooks be sent to China to assist in organizing a presbytery. That fall, Texas Synod took the necessary steps to order the organization of Canton Presbytery, commissioning the Reverend D. W. Fooks and the Reverend Gam Sing Quah for this purpose. They received two ordained ministers from other denominations and ordained still another. The organization of Canton Presbytery took place on October 24, 1924. Seven churches with a total membership of 1,035 were represented in this meeting.

In the fall of 1929, Samuel King Gam, eldest son of Gam Sing Quah, came to America to enter Bethel College. In 1931, Gam Sing Quah came to America for the last time. Samuel King Gam returned to China in 1935 to work among the young people and to supervise the social and educational programs of the mission. Larger responsibilities were soon to be his, however, for early in 1937 Gam Sing Quah departed this life, leaving the superintendency of the Chinese missions to fall on his son's shoulders.

Soon thereafter began the Sino-Japanese War. During the summer of 1938, the Canton church and the Gam home were twice bombed. Samuel King Gam sent his family to Macau, a Portuguese colony. About this time McAdow Gam, his younger brother, entered Bethel College to prepare to become a social worker. In the fall of 1938, Canton was taken over by the Japanese. By early 1939, eight of the ten missions were closed. Samuel King Gam began work at Hong Kong and Macau, but shortly thereafter returned to Canton and directed relief work. A boys' home was established under his direction. In June, 1942, Samuel

King Gam again escaped from Canton, but Hong Kong also fell to the Japanese. In June, 1943, McAdow Gam returned to China where he became assistant to E. H. Lockwood, executive chairman of the Church Committee for China Relief, in Kwangtung.

Following the close of World War II, plans were made for rebuilding what had been lost in China. In June, 1946, a new chapel in Canton was dedicated. Plans for a Gam Sing Quah Memorial Fund were begun. In 1949, however, the Communists obtained control of Peking and soon thereafter occupied the entire Chinese mainland. Schools and hospitals became government property. A "bamboo curtain" was drawn.

The Gam family now transferred their activities to Hong Kong and Macau. Many refugees came from the mainland. In October, 1951, Samuel King Gam and his family came to the United States, leaving McAdow Gam to direct the work at Hong Kong and Macau. In 1952, McAdow came to the United States and was ordained to the ministry by Lebanon Presbytery.

The work at Macau and Hong Kong has been carried on mainly among the less privileged people. Upon McAdow's return to Hong Kong, work was begun among the "boat people." One man who was converted to Christianity offered his boat as a place to conduct evangelistic services. Later a place was rented on the island of Cheung Chau. Schools were held on the rooftops of government-built resettlement houses. During the year 1959, youth work was begun in Kowloon, a section of Hong Kong. During the year, the Hong Kong church was dedicated and a building was purchased at Macau.

The work begun under the leadership of Gam Sing Quah in China has been conducted exclusively by Chinese leadership. In 1963, Paul Hom, who entered the ministry from the Chinese Church in San Francisco, was sent to Hong Kong to assist McAdow Gam.

COLOMBIA, SOUTH AMERICA

As early as 1913, there were young people in the Cumberland Presbyterian Church who were interested in missions in South America. In 1922, the Woman's Board of Missions accepted as candidates for that field the Reverend and Mrs. Walter L. Swartz. In May, 1925, they were commissioned. In November, 1925, Swartz sailed from New York to seek a location for the projected mission. Colombia, where there were only thirty Protestant missionaries among seven million people, was chosen. He was encouraged in this choice by the Reverend C. P. Chapman of the Christian and Missionary Alliance who was laboring at Cali. In March, 1926, Mrs. Swartz joined her husband, and on April 1 a house was rented.

The first person baptized was a boy named Jose Fajardo whose brother, Martiniano Fajardo, had recently accepted Christ in a Protestant service at Palmira. Both became ministers of the gospel.

In 1928, Misses Bernice Barnett and Ethel Brintle were sent to Colombia, and that fall the Colegio Americano was opened in Cali with twenty-eight students, one of whom was Jose Fajardo. On February 4, 1929, the Cali church was organized with four Colombian families, about fifteen members in all. Preaching points were established at Dagua, Lomitas, and El Pinal. Another point visited by the missionaries was La Helvecia, near Armenia, where a church had been begun and later abandoned by another denomination. This church is said to have been the first Protestant church in Colombia to employ its own pastor and pay his salary. In 1933, this church called Alfredo Cardona as its pastor. Work was also begun at Pereira where property was purchased from the Plymouth Brethren who had begun a work there in 1924.

On March 8, 1935, Cauca Valley Presbytery was organized by order of Texas Synod. Three ordained ministers were present, and there were four churches represented.

There have been many changes in personnel through the years, but the work has continued to make progress. A persecution politically conceived and often encouraged by the Roman Catholic clergy was begun in 1948 and greatly intensified in 1950. Churches at El Pinal and Restrepo were burned. An attempt was made to dynamite the church at Dagua. In general, the work had to be shifted from the rural sections to the larger towns. Since the revolution which took place in May, 1957, conditions have been more conducive to the progress of Protestant missions.

On March 14, 1961, the Colegio Americano became accredited by the Department of Education of Colombia. It has the distinction of being the only co-educational colegio in Colombia and the only school approved by the government which does not teach the Catholic religion.

Over the years, a number of North Americans have served in the mission in Colombia. The present staff includes lay personnel as well as ministers.

RE-ENTRY INTO JAPAN

At the close of World War II, Japan was spiritually bankrupt. Shintoism could no longer meet the needs of the Japanese people. In this spiritual vacuum, the chaplains of the occupying American forces were of great help.

In January, 1948, the Reverend Tadao Yoshizaki, a Baptist minister who had been working in China, visited Chaplain Cleetis C. Clemens to request help for the people of his community. On the second Sunday afternoon, Clemens preached to six Japanese, and Tadao interpreted. In February a fund to erect a mission building was started at the Zama base where Chaplain Clemens was stationed. The group at the mission became a Cumberland Presbyterian church with Tadao Yoshizaki as pastor. Subsequently, the Board of Foreign Missions accepted the mission field with the Koza community church as a mission point. The Koza church is located in Yamatomachi, a town of two thousand inhabitants, where General MacArthur first set foot upon Japan at the close of the war. The church was received under the care of California Presbytery in August, 1950. By this time the church program included Sunday school, morning worship, prayer meeting, youth meetings, women's society, kindergarten, English Bible study, English study class, and Bible study class. There were more than two hundred in Sunday school and eighty in kindergarten.

Soon the church began to reach out into the surrounding areas. In November, 1952, the Reverend and Mrs. Thomas Forester were commissioned as missionaries to Japan. In 1961, the Reverend and Mrs. Tolbert Dill were sent to this field. The Foresters returned to the United States in 1964, and the Reverend and Mrs. Melvin D. Stott, Jr., were sent to the Japanese field. Meanwhile work has been started at Shibusawa, Kiboga Oka, Kunitachi, and Higashi Koganei.

SOMETHING TO THINK ABOUT

1. Why did the earliest foreign missionary efforts of the Cumberland Presbyterian Church fail?

2. What was the original purpose of the organization of a Woman's Board of Missions? What changes in function and constituency has this board undergone in the course of the years?

3. What was the status of the foreign mission work of the Cumberland Presbyterian Church in 1906 as to fields occupied, number of missionaries, number of organized churches, and membership on mission fields? What is the status of this work today?

4. Of the foreign missions attempted by the Cumberland Presbyterian Church, which were the result of deliberate planning? Which were opened up through unexpected, yet seemingly providential, means?

5. What role has education (i.e., the founding of schools on the mission fields) played in the foreign mission work of the Cumberland Presbyterian Church? Why is educational work considered important?

6. Can a church exist and fulfill its purpose without engaging in missions? in missions in foreign lands? Why?

8. The Church Founds Educational Institutions

IN THE LETTER addressed by the Council of Revival Ministers to the General Assembly of the Presbyterian Church in 1807, the following affirmation was made on the subject of education: "We never have embraced the idea of an unlearned ministry. The peculiar state of our country and extent of the revival, reduced us to the necessity of introducing more of that description than we otherwise would. We sincerely esteem a learned and pious ministry, and hope that the church will never be left destitute of such an ornament."

ATTITUDE OF THE FOUNDERS

In the "Circular Letter" sent out by the Cumberland Presbytery soon after its organization in 1810 the following statements appear:

"Some fear lest the Presbytery should take too much liberty in licensing and ordaining unlearned men. If by this you mean, you are afraid the Presbytery, in some instances, will dispense with the dead languages, your fears are well grounded. But if you are afraid we will license and ordain men without a good English education, we hope your fears are without foundation."

The new presbytery, in fact, demonstrated its concern for the education of its ministers in at least three ways. First, it set up standards which had to be met preparatory to ordination. In the compact entered into on February 4, 1810, on the occasion of the organization of the new presbytery, the following requirements were set forth: "Moreover, all licentiates before they are set apart to the whole work of the ministry, or ordained, shall be required to undergo an examination on English Grammar, Geography, Astronomy, Natural and Moral Philosophy, and Church History. The Presbytery may also require an examination on all, or any part, of the above branches of literature before licensure if they deem it expedient." A footnote explains that "It will not be understood that examinations on experimental religion and Theology will be omitted." An examination of the records of the Cumberland Presbytery during its three and a half years of existence prior to the organization of the Cumberland Synod reveals that the presbytery faithfully lived up to these requirements. Each man whose ordination is recorded was examined prior to his ordination on the subjects mentioned.

Second, the presbytery sought to improve the educational status of its ministers, licentiates, and candidates by purchasing and maintaining a circulating library. The resolution establishing the Cumberland Presbytery Library was passed in March, 1811. Each ordained minister, licentiate, and candidate was asked to contribute five dollars for this purpose. A total of fifty-four dollars was raised at this meeting of presbytery, and by the next regular meeting of presbytery in October a number of books had been purchased. Among the books purchased were Campbell's *Lectures,* Ferguson's *Astronomy,* Addison's *Evidences,* Watt's *Logic, Manners and Customs, Study of the Bible,* Stewart's *Philosophy, Natural Philosophy,* and Guthrie's *Grammar.* Other contributions were made to the library fund and additional books purchased later. These books were distributed among the ordained ministers, licentiates, and candidates at each regular meeting of presbytery and were returned at the next meeting. When it was decided to form a synod, the books and money belonging to the Cumberland Presbytery Library were divided among the three presbyteries.

Third, the presbytery gave direct financial aid to ministerial candidates who were in position to attend school. In October, 1811, the presbytery adopted the following resolution:

> "Resolved, That for the purpose of educating Philip McDaniel, the ordained ministers present, do mutually agree and bind themselves to collect or procure ten dollars, and as much more as they can, for the above purpose, and if there should be any more money raised than will be necessary, it shall be applied to similar purposes by the direction of Presbytery; one-half the money to be collected at least by our next Presbytery, the balance by our next fall session."

In November, 1812, it was reported "that the whole demand against the Presbytery for said McDaniel's tuition and board is fifty-seven dollars and ten cents." The few dollars that were lacking were immediately contributed and the obligation met in full.

These further evidences of the interest of the founders of the Cumberland Presbyterian Church in education are worthy of notice: In the winter of 1821-1822, Finis Ewing established a school at his home at New Lebanon, Cooper County, Missouri, for the education of the candidates for the ministry in McGee Presbytery. He boarded them in his home without charge and instructed them in theology, while R. D. Morrow gave them instruction in literature and science. Dr. Beard says, "This was the first movement toward a Theological School in the Cumberland Presbyterian Church, and, I suppose, west of the Mississippi River." [1] It was for this group of candidates that Ewing prepared his *Lectures on the Most Important Subjects in Divinity.*

When the question of establishing a college was before the Synod in 1825, Ewing made a speech which Dr. Cossitt afterward said was "the most lucid and powerful argument in favor of ministerial education, to which the writer ever listened." Dr. Cossitt, who was president of the denomination's first college, goes on to point out that Ewing "was always one of the warmest friends and most liberal patrons of this institution." Ewing directed that the profits from his lectures go to Cumberland College. Subsequently, when Cumberland College was in sore financial straits, he prepared for publication an appeal to the entire church in which he proposed to make a donation of $250 toward the first $50,000, and a like donation toward the second $50,000 that the church would raise as a permanent endowment fund for the college." The last letter Dr. Cossitt ever received from Ewing contained subscriptions which Ewing had obtained for the endowment of Cumberland College in the amount of $1,125. [2]

The Reverend D. W. McLin rendered in Illinois a service similar to that which Ewing rendered in Missouri. Dr. J. B. Logan says, "Rev. David W. McLin—who, perhaps more than any other man, gave shape to the early operations of the Church in Illinois, founded a school at his own house or in his neighborhood, where he taught candidates for the ministry." He goes on to list several candidates whom McLin taught. This was in about the year 1824 at Enfield, White County.[3]

Samuel King and Robert Donnell each traveled, at different times, as financial agents for Cumberland College. Robert Donnell was a leader in getting Cumberland University located at Lebanon and gave lectures on theology in this institution while he was serving as pastor of the church in Lebanon.

Thomas Calhoun had a son who entered the ministry. He sent his son to college and later to a theological school. Concerning Calhoun, Dr. McDonnold says, "He nearly all his life was aiding some young preacher to obtain a college education." [4]

In 1820, a mission school was established among the Chickasaw Indians near the present site of Aberdeen, Mississippi. Of the three men who represented the church in working out the agreement with the Indian chiefs for founding the school, two (Samuel King and Robert Bell) were members of the first presbytery of the Cumberland Presbyterian Church. From 1820 until 1832, this school, which was known as Charity Hall, was conducted by the Reverend and Mrs. Robert Bell.

CUMBERLAND COLLEGE

The first college founded by the Cumberland Presbyterian Church was provided for by a resolution of the Cumberland Synod adopted October 22, 1825. Five commissioners were appointed to select a site, receive donations and subscriptions, purchase land, and make the necessary arrangements for bringing the institution into operation. A tract of land consisting of not less than two hundred nor more than five hundred acres was to be purchased, and every student was to be employed in manual labor not less than two nor more than three hours a day. Produce of the farm was expected to be appropriated by the boarding establishment. Feather beds were forbidden, and students were to be restricted to a frugal and wholesome diet, "avoiding all luxuries." Tuition was set at thirty dollars per year. There was to be no charge for boarding and washing, unless the necessities of the institution should require it, and in any case the charge was not to exceed thirty dollars per year. The board of trustees was also authorized to establish a printing office to publish a periodical paper, books, tracts, et cetera, if deemed expedient.

The commission met in January, 1826, and visited Princeton, Hopkinsville, Elkton, and Russellville, Kentucky, all of which had made proposals with a view to securing the location of the school. Princeton was selected, and a farm of between four and five hundred acres was purchased. Unfortunately, many of the subscriptions which had been offered for the location of the school were never paid. Money had to be borrowed to make the down payment for the farm.

The first president of the school was the Reverend Franceway Ranna Cossitt. Born at Claremont, New Hampshire, April 24, 1790, he was graduated from Middlebury College, in Vermont, in 1813. He studied theology at New Haven (which later became the General Episcopal Seminary of New York), and he was licensed as a lay reader in the Protestant Episcopal Church. Later he went to Tennessee and taught school near Clarksville. In the summer of 1821, he came in contact with, and was attracted to, the Cumberland Presbyterian Church. He was received by Logan Presbytery as a licentiate in October, 1821, and was ordained by Anderson Presbytery the following year. Dr. Cossitt was one of the leaders in the founding of the college, and the manual labor aspect was his idea.

The college was chartered as Cumberland College. By 1830 there were about 125 students, all young men, as the college was never coeducational. Dr. Richard Beard, who entered Cumberland

College in 1830, says, "The college seemed a good deal like a bee-hive. Each teacher was ringing the bell every hour for his class; and every two hours the horn was blowing for the laboring divisions." [5]

In an attempt to solve the ever-present financial difficulties of the school, the college property was leased in 1831 to the Reverend John Barnett and Aaron Shelby. Shelby sold his interest to a Mr. Young who died shortly thereafter, and the trustees became a partner with Barnett in the enterprise. In 1837, a joint stock association was formed to assume the debts of the school and provide for its operation. About 1839, the subject of transferring the school to some other Christian denomination was considered. The General Assembly adopted plans in 1840 for the raising of $100,000 for educational purposes of which $55,000 was to be endowment for Cumberland College, but the plans were only partially carried out, and there was only temporary relief. The next General Assembly, meeting in 1842, resolved to move the school to a more promising location. This resolution, as will be seen, resulted in the founding of Cumberland University, at Lebanon, Tennessee.

Cumberland College was continued, however, under the auspices of Green River Synod. From 1843 until 1854, Richard Beard served as president. The farm was sold with the exception of ten acres on which were the college buildings. The operation of the college was continued until June, 1860.

Throughout its history Cumberland College was plagued by financial difficulties arising from the failure of the church to give its support. Nonetheless, it made a distinct contribution to education. A beginning was made toward a scientific teaching of agriculture. We are told that as early as 1837 "The college set aside about twenty acres of ground which was prepared and cultivated as the faculty may direct for making agricultural experiments and elucidating the science of husbandry and gardening." It was intended that students attending the institution should "carry a knowledge of scientific agriculture back to their home community and improve agricultural practices there." [6]

Furthermore, a number of men who became educators in the

Cumberland Presbyterian Church or elsewhere received their college education here. Among these may be mentioned Dr. Richard Beard, who became the first professor of systematic theology in the theological school at Cumberland University; Dr. B. W. McDonnold, who served as president of Bethel College and later of Cumberland University; Dr. S. G. Burney, who became Dr. Beard's successor as professor of theology at Cumberland University; and Dr. W. A. Scott, one of the founders of the San Francisco Theological Seminary of the Presbyterian Church, U. S. A.

CUMBERLAND UNIVERSITY

In May, 1842, the General Assembly appointed a committee to receive bids for the relocation of its college. The proposal submitted by Lebanon, Tennessee, to provide a site and $10,000 in cash for the erection of a building, was accepted. A board of trustees was appointed. This board selected Dr. F. R. Cossitt, who up until this time had served as president of the college at Princeton, as president of the school which soon became known as Cumberland University.

From the beginning the school had the support of the citizens of Lebanon, one of the most liberal of whom was Robert L. Caruthers who for forty years served as a trustee. A law school was established in 1847, and Judge Abram Caruthers became the first professor, his salary being guaranteed by his brother, Robert L. Caruthers. This school opened with seven students, but during the first year twenty-five were enrolled. By 1857-1858 there were 181 students. Concerning the law school Dr. B. W. McDonnold wrote:

> "From the first the law school has combined all the best methods of instruction with the services of the very ablest professors. The instruction does not consist of mere lectures by those who have turned aside for an hour from busy practice at the bar, but able lawyers give their whole time to the classes, teaching by recitations, lectures, and moot courts." [7]

A school of engineering was established in 1852. Professor A. P. Stewart, a graduate of the U. S. Military Academy and later a general in the army of the Confederate States of America, was the first head of this school.

In the early years of the university, lectures in theology were given by the Reverend Robert Donnell and the Reverend David Lowry, pastors of the Lebanon church, and by Dr. T. C. Anderson, second president of the University. In 1852, the General Assembly voted to establish a theological school at Cumberland University. This school was opened in March, 1854, with Dr. Richard Beard as the only professor. From 1854 until 1858, the number of strictly theological students ranged from four to seven, although candidates for the ministry attending the College of Arts attended the theological lectures also. In 1859, Dr. B. W. McDonnold was appointed professor of Pastoral Theology and Sacred Rhetoric. In 1861, the work of the theological school, as well as that of the entire university, was interrupted by the War Between the States.

In 1877, three men were inaugurated as professors in the Theological School: Dr. W. H. Darnall, professor of Church History; Dr. S. G. Burney, professor of Biblical Literature; and Dr. R. V. Foster, professor of Hebrew and New Testament Greek. Following Dr. Beard's death in 1880, Dr. Burney and Dr. Foster served successively as professors of systematic theology. Other professors who served prior to the closing of the theological school in 1909 included Dr. J. D. Kirkpatrick (1878-1895) and Dr. J. V. Stephens (1896-1909) in Church History; Dr. Claiborne H. Bell (1884-1909) in Missions and Comparative Religions; Dr. J. M. Hubbert (1893-1902), Homiletics and Pastoral Theology; Dr. W. P. Bone (1894-1909), New Testament Interpretation; Dr. Finis King Farr (1895-1909), Hebrew and Old Testament Interpretation; and Dr. R. G. Pearson (1903-1909), English Bible and Evangelistic Methods. From the beginning of the Theological School in 1854 until its discontinuance in 1909, 430 D.D. degrees were conferred by Cumberland University.

Concerning the contribution of Cumberland University, Dr. W. P. Bone has written:

> "It would be impossible to include all of Cumberland's alumni who have attained positions of eminence or

who have rendered distinguished service. An incomplete list recently made is as follows: College and university presidents, 47; college and university professors, 106; moderators of church national assemblies, 21; Justices, United States Supreme Court, 2; United State Senators, 9; Congressmen, 66; Federal District Judges, 10; Federal Circuit Judges, 4; Federal District Attorneys, 12; Generals, 8; Governors, 11; State Supreme Judges, 42; Judges, Court of Appeals, 12; State Attorney Generals, 14; Chancellors, 20; District Judges, 65; United States Ministers, 4; Secretary of State, 1; other high positions, 50." [8]

Cumberland University passed from under the control of the Cumberland Presbyterian Church in 1906.

OTHER EDUCATIONAL INSTITUTIONS

Early in its history the Cumberland Presbyterian Church envisioned a comprehensive program of education for the masses. Many of its early ministers on the frontier were also teachers. One General Assembly recommended a school system to embrace "schools in the bounds of every congregation," "a presbyterial school in the bounds of every presbytery," these to be "crowned by the university at Lebanon and the colleges at Princeton, Beverly, and Uniontown." [9] Under this sort of program numerous schools were launched. Many presbyteries resolved to establish schools. Those which survived were eventually taken under the care of some synod. In time the need for co-operation from a larger area was seen, and several synods co-operated in establishing a college or university of respectable standing. The trend toward such co-operative efforts did not take place everywhere at the same time. Nor were the efforts at establishing local and presbyterial schools fruitless, for often these were the earliest schools established in the communities in which they were located. They met a need.

What happened in the subsequent development of the program of higher education may be illustrated as follows:

Prior to 1849, three schools had been operated in Ohio and Pennsylvania for longer or shorter periods of time, more or less under the auspices of the Cumberland Presbyterian Church. These were Madison College, Uniontown, Pennsylvania, which came under Cumberland Presbyterian influence in 1835; Beverly College, Beverly, Ohio, which in 1843 had been placed under the care of Pennsylvania Synod; and Greene Academy, Carmichaels, Pennsylvania. Madison College has the distinction of having been one of the earliest colleges in the United States to be co-educational. Since none of these schools continued to operate successfully, Pennsylvania Presbytery, in 1849, resolved to found a school within its bounds. Waynesburg was the place chosen. In November, 1851, the school was opened in its new building. By March, 1850, a charter had been procured providing that Pennsylvania Presbytery would appoint four of the seven trustees contingent upon its maintaining three professorships. Shortly thereafter this responsibility was taken over by Pennsylvania Synod.

In 1850, a female school had been created under the name of Waynesburg Female Seminary. In the fall of 1851 both schools were conducted in the new building, and men and women attended many of the same classes. By 1858, the male and female departments had been combined into one college.

The first class was graduated from the college in September, 1853. Among the members of this class was A. B. Miller who immediately was named a teacher in the school and in 1859 was made president. Under his administration, which was a lengthy one, Waynesburg College continued to prosper.

Among the early schools in Illinois may be mentioned Ewing Seminary, founded in 1843, first under the care of Illinois Presbytery and later of Illinois Synod; Stout's Grove Seminary, founded in 1849 by Mackinaw Presbytery; Le Roy Seminary, 1852, a continuation of Stout's Grove Seminary; Sullivan Academy, 1851; Union College, Virginia, Illinois, 1851, sponsored first by Sangamon Presbytery and later by Sangamon and Illinois Synods; and Mt. Zion Seminary, which was accepted by Decatur Presbytery in 1865. In the meantime, however, a proposal had arisen in Indiana to establish a college on a co-operative basis to serve the states of Indiana, Illinois, and Iowa. Just at that time the need for a college for the education of ministers was most urgent because of the plight of the colleges in the South as a result of the war. Thus five synods—Indiana, Iowa, Illinois, Central Illinois, and Sangamon—co-operated in the founding of Lincoln University at Lincoln, Illinois. This school opened in November, 1866. Among the most prominent persons connected with this institution were the first three presidents: the Reverend Azel Freeman, D.D., the Reverend J. C. Bowdon, D.D., and the Reverend A. J. McGlumphy, D.D.

In Texas a similar decision to act on a co-operative basis was made just after the close of the War Between the States. Prior to the war three schools had been sponsored by the Cumberland Presbyterian Church in Texas. La Grange Collegiate Institute (later known as Ewing College) began its first session in 1848 under the supervision of Colorado Presbytery. In the fall of 1859 it became a synodical school under the care of Colorado Synod. Chapel Hill College, Daingerfield, Texas, was founded by Marshall Presbytery in the fall of 1849 or spring of 1850. It came under the care of Texas Synod in August, 1854. Larissa College was begun as an enterprise of Trinity Presbytery but was at once adopted as a synodical school by Brazos Synod. All three of these schools were closed during the war. One or two of them were reopened briefly after the war, but the movement to establish a school to serve the three synods was getting under way.

In 1867 committees were appointed by the Texas, Brazos, and Colorado Synods looking to the establishment of one central school. The school was located at Tehuacana, Texas (although several other places, including Dallas, had made proposals for its location). The school was opened September 23, 1869, and was named Trinity University. The first president was Dr. W. E. Beeson, who had previously served as president of Chapel Hill College at Daingerfield. In 1902, Trinity was moved to Waxahachie. In 1942, it was moved to San Antonio, where it continues as a school of the United Presbyterian Church, U. S. A.

McGee College, College Mound, Missouri, was closed in 1874 because of inadequate financial support. It was sponsored first by McGee Presbytery and later by McAdow Synod. On October 27, 1874, an Educational Commission was formed consisting of elected personnel from the Synods of McAdow, Mis-

souri, and Ozark. It was decided that an endowment of at least
$100,000 must be raised before another school would be
attempted.[10] Subsequently the Synod of Kansas co-operated in the
undertaking. In 1888, Marshall, Missouri, was chosen as the site
of the new school, which was called Missouri Valley College.
From the beginning the college was co-educational. It opened
September 17, 1889, with 153 students enrolled during the first
year. Dr. William H. Black became the first president in 1890.

In 1900, Mr. James Millikin, of Decatur, Illinois, offered
a gift for the establishment of an institution in Decatur under
conditions which were met by the citizens of that community and
the Synods of Illinois, Indiana, and Iowa of the Cumberland Presbyterian Church. In April, 1901, the charter of Lincoln University
was amended so as to change the name to Lincoln College and
merge it with the new college at Decatur as the James Millikin
University. The school at Decatur was opened in 1903. In addition
to the schools already mentioned, there were within the Cumberland Presbyterian Church in 1906 several other schools of which
Arkansas Cumberland College, Clarksville, Arkansas, and Bethel
College, McKenzie, Tennessee, were the strongest.

A movement had been begun in 1899 to raise a million
dollars in educational endowment for the schools and colleges of
the Cumberland Presbyterian Church by 1910, the centennial of
the Church. As a result of the attempted union in 1906, however,
all of these schools passed into the control of the Presbyterian
Church, U. S. A. However, the board of trustees of Bethel College, which was under the control of West Tennessee Synod,
adhered to the Cumberland Presbyterian Church, maintained a
rival school until a favorable decree was obtained relative to the
college property, and thenceforth continued the operation of
Bethel College as a Cumberland Presbyterian school.

Of the schools established by the Cumberland Presbyterian
Church which passed into the hands of the Presbyterian Church,
U. S. A., in 1906, Waynesburg College, Lincoln College (which
again became a separate institution in 1953), James Millikin
University, Missouri Valley College, and the College of the Ozarks
(formerly Arkansas Cumberland College) continue as schools of

the United Presbyterian Church, U. S. A. The Cumberland University Law School was moved to Birmingham, Alabama, in 1961, and is now being operated as the Cumberland School of Law of Howard College.

Dr. H. B. Evans found reference to no less than eighty-four educational institutions which have been at one time or another sponsored by the Cumberland Presbyterian Church.[11] The total number of such institutions is probably nearer one hundred. Thus the interest of Cumberland Presbyterians in education has received abundant testimony.

SOMETHING TO THINK ABOUT

1. What evidences are there that Cumberland Presbyterian ministers of the first generation were interested in education?

2. What values were to be found in manual labor colleges such as Cumberland College was intended to be? What were the disadvantages of such a plan?

3. Why was Cumberland College so often in financial difficulties? Why was Cumberland University more successful in this respect?

4. What lessons were learned from the attempt to establish a multiplicity of schools? How did the major colleges of the denomination which were in existence in 1906 come into being?

5. Why is Bethel College the only college now owned and supported by the Cumberland Presbyterian Church?

9. The Church Develops Its Confession of Faith

ATTENTION HAS ALREADY been given to the difficulty which arose in the Synod of Kentucky of the Presbyterian Church over Cumberland Presbytery's permitting its candidates for the ministry at their licensure and ordination to accept the Westminster Confession of Faith only insofar as they considered it consistent with the Word of God. The real difficulty, of course, was over the acceptance of the doctrine of unconditional predestination as stated in the Westminster Confession. The experiences of the revival, in which it was evident that the Holy Spirit was working in the masses and that men never before suspected of being among the elect were crying out for mercy, must have led the participants to question a doctrinal scheme which seemed to teach that salvation was designed only for a select few.

Thus there came into being a theological system which was not the product of the logic of Scholasticism but of the intense fervor of an evangelical awakening. The theological position of Cumberland Presbyterians was not conceived by logicians but by evangelists.

THE PRESBYTERIAN CONFESSION ADOPTED

The first official doctrinal statement of the new church was contained in the compact which was entered into in the reorganization of Cumberland Presbytery. It was as follows:

> "All candidates for the ministry, who may hereafter be licensed by this Presbytery, and all the licentiates or probationers, who may hereafter be ordained by this Presbytery, shall be required, before such licensure and ordination, to receive and adopt the Confession and Discipline of the Presbyterian Church, except the idea of fatality, that seems to be taught under the mysterious doctrine of predestination. It is to be understood, however, that such as can clearly receive the Confession, without an exception, shall not be required to make any."

The purpose of this provision was simply to guarantee to those who should unite with the new presbytery the liberty which the members of the presbytery had sought and had failed to obtain in the Presbyterian Church. No further creedal statement was drawn up at the time, since the members of the new presbytery still entertained hope for a reunion with the Presbyterian Church.

A BRIEF STATEMENT IS DRAWN UP

As soon as it became apparent that the anticipated reunion with the main body of Presbyterians was not going to take place, it became increasingly necessary for the members of Cumberland Presbytery to state their position before the world. Accordingly, at the last meeting of Cumberland Presbytery prior to its division to form three presbyteries, a committee consisting of Finis Ewing and Robert Donnell was appointed "to draw up a complete, though succinct, account of the rise, doctrines, etc., of the Cumberland Presbytery." This committee was directed to report to the synod which was to be constituted at Beech meetinghouse, Sumner County, Tennessee, in October, 1813.

The report of this committee was adopted at the first meeting of the Cumberland Synod and was directed to be published in Woodward's edition of Buck's *Theological Dictionary*. As to doctrines, this statement sets forth six essential doctrines held by Cumberland Presbyterians, four points on which they dissent from the Presbyterian Confession, and a statement to the effect that Cumberland Presbyterians claim to hold a "middle ground" between Calvinism and Arminianism.

The grounds of dissent from the Westminster Confession are stated in the following paragraph:

> "They dissent from the Confession—in, 1st, That there are no *eternal* reprobates.—2nd, That Christ died not for a *part only,* but for *all* mankind.—3rd, That all infants, dying in infancy, are saved through Christ and sanctification of the Spirit.—4th, That the Spirit of God operates on the *world,* or as coextensively as Christ has made the atonement, in such a manner as to leave all men inexcusable."

At this same meeting of synod a committee was appointed to prepare a Confession of Faith, Catechism, and Discipline. This committee consisted of William McGee, Finis Ewing, Robert Donnell, and Thomas Calhoun, all ministers.

THE CONFESSION OF 1814

The committee named above made its report to the synod in its 1814 meeting, and, although there were some amendments, the final vote on every item was unanimous.

This Confession of Faith followed the plan of the Westminster Confession. Many whole chapters were adopted almost verbatim. Other chapters were materially changed by additions or omissions, or by a rewriting of a section to make it harmonize with the belief and teachings of Cumberland Presbyterians. The principal changes made were in Chapters III, VIII, X, XIII, and XVII, although there were minor changes in several other chapters.

In Chapter III, "The Decrees of God," the Westminster Confession of Faith states that God from eternity ordained "whatsoever comes to pass." The Confession adopted by the Cumberland Synod in 1814 stated that God determined to bring to pass "what should be for his own glory." The section relative to the passing by of the non-elect was omitted as was also the section declaring that the number of the elect "is so certain and definite that it cannot be either increased or diminished."

Chapter VIII of the Westminster Confession states that through Christ's sacrifice of himself he "purchased not only reconciliation, but an everlasting-inheritance in the kingdom of heaven, for all those whom the Father hath given unto him." The last clause was changed to read "for all those who come to the Father by him." The final section of this chapter was changed so as to contain a clear statement that "Jesus Christ, by the grace of God, has tasted death for every man."

The doctrine of "Effectual Calling" (chapter X) begins with the statement, "All those whom God hath predestinated unto life, and those only, he is pleased, in his appointed and accepted time, effectually to call. . . ." Cumberland Presbyterians changed this statement to read, "All those whom God calls, *and who obey the call,* and those only, he is pleased by his word and Spirit to bring out of that state of sin and death in which they are by nature, to grace and salvation by Jesus Christ." Instead of the statement, "Elect infants, dying in infancy, are regenerated and saved by Christ through the Spirit," Cumberland Presbyterians affirmed that "All infants dying in infancy are regenerated and saved by Christ, through the Spirit."

Instead of stating, under the head "Perseverance of the Saints," that those who are effectually called "can neither totally nor finally fall away from the state of grace," Cumberland Presbyterians substituted the following: "They whom God hath justified and sanctified, he will also glorify; consequently, the *truly* regenerated soul will never totally nor finally fall away from the state of grace, but shall certainly persevere therein to the end, and be eternally saved." Cumberland Presbyterians refused to base this doctrine on "the immutability of the decree of election," as does the Westminster Confession, although they followed the older Confession in basing it upon "the unchangeable love and power of God; the merits, advocacy, and intercession of Jesus Christ, the abiding of the Spirit and seed of God within them; and the nature of the covenant of grace."

In the third section of this chapter, the Westminster Confession mentions the possibility that those who have been accepted by God, effectually called and sanctified may "fall into grievous sins" and "hurt and scandalize others, and bring temporal judgements upon themselves." This section was changed by Cumberland Presbyterians to read as follows:

> "Although there are examples in the Old Testament of good men having egregiously sinned, and some of them continuing for a time therein; yet now, since life and immortality are brought clearer to light by the gospel, and especially since the effusion of the Holy Ghost on the day of Pentecost, we may not expect the true Christian to fall into such gross sins. Nevertheless, they may, through the temptations of Satan, the world, and the flesh, the neglect of the means of grace, fall into sin and incur God's displeasure, and grieve his Holy Spirit; come to be deprived of some measure of their graces and comforts, and have their consciences wounded; but the real Christian can never rest satisfied therein."

Although the synod "remodeled" the Westminster Confession according to its own interpretation of the Scriptures, that confession was declared to be "in the main, an admirable work, especially to have been framed so shortly after the Roman superstition and idolatry had almost covered the whole Christian world." At the same time the synod claimed the right "to adopt what they think right, and expunge what they think erroneous, from any *human creed.*"

THE CONFESSION OF 1883

No change was made in 1814 in the order of subjects as found in the Westminster Confession. Furthermore, it was impossible, simply by expunging words, phrases, or even whole sections, to eliminate all the implications of a system which was founded on the view that God had designed to save only a select portion of mankind. This doctrine permeated much of the Westminster Confession from Chapter III onward.

As early as 1852, agitation was begun in the General Assembly for a revision of the Confession of Faith. The vote on this question that year, however, was decidedly in the negative. In 1853, a committee prepared and presented a proposed creed which included a rearrangement of the order of the chapters and some verbal changes. Again the vote of the General Assembly was in the negative.

The revisionists persisted, however, and in 1881 a memorial was presented to the General Assembly from Tehuacana Presbytery asking for a revision of the Confession of Faith. This memorial received favorable consideration, and two committees were appointed, one to revise the book and the other to review and revise the work of the first committee. The result of the work of the committees was published and distributed in pamphlet form so that the committees might have the benefit of any suggestions or criticisms before making their report to the Assembly. The next General Assembly resolved itself into a committee of the whole, and the proposed revision was considered item by item. Some changes were made, and the proposed book, as amended, was submitted to the presbyteries for their acceptance or rejection. Coupled with the transmission of the book to the presbyteries was the following provision:

"It being hereby distinctly understood and declared that those who have heretofore received and adopted the Confession of Faith approved by the General Assembly in 1829, and who prefer to adhere to the doctrinal statements contained therein, are at liberty to do so." McDonnold says, "This item went far toward satisfying the anti-revisionists." [1] Through oversight, or for some unknown cause, this paragraph was omitted from the stereotyped book, but it stands as the decision of the church nevertheless.

The vote on the adoption of the new book was almost unanimous, and in 1883, when the vote was tabulated, it was formally declared "that the Confession of Faith and Government of the Cumberland Presbyterian Church had been constitutionally changed, and that the Revised Confession, as approved by the Presbyteries, is hereafter to be of binding authority upon the churches."

The committees, in submitting the result of their labors to the General Assembly in 1882, made the following statement concerning the policy to which they adhered in framing the new Confession:

"Mindful of the fact that the Committees were appointed, not to make a new Confession, but to revise the old one, we have studied not to transcend our authority, and we have no hesitation in saying that we have not changed a single doctrine fundamental to your scheme of theology, or any of its logical correlates.

"We have attempted to draw with precision the boundaries between your theological scheme and those of other Churches, and then to allow the utmost liberty of opinion within these bounds. Hence, we have not sought to put into this revision tenets peculiar to any man, but only such as are common to all, and we think we have so far succeeded in this endeavor as that every intelligent Cumberland Presbyterian can cheerfully subscribe to all that is set forth in the revision." [2]

From the foregoing it may be seen that (1) the new book was considered by its authors to be a revision rather than a new Confession; (2) it was intended to set forth only what was generally believed and preached throughout the church; and (3) liberty of opinion was to be indulged within the limits laid down.

If one compares this edition of the Confession of Faith with the Confession of 1814, it will be found that the principal changes consisted in:

Rearrangement of Material. The revisers added two new subjects, "Regeneration" and "Growth in Grace," to give emphasis to doctrines preached by Cumberland Presbyterians which it was felt were inadequately treated in the older Confession. Two important changes in chapter headings were made: "Divine Influence" was substituted for "Effectual Calling," and "Preservation of Believers" for "Perseverance of the Saints." The order of subjects, one of the greatest sources of dissatisfaction with the Confession of 1814, was changed. The following table shows the order followed in the new Confession as compared with that found in the old (which was the same as in the Westminster Confession), chapters X-XV:

Confession of 1814	Confession of 1883
Effectual Calling	Divine Influence
Justification	Repentance unto Life
Adoption	Saving Faith
Sanctification	Justification
Saving Faith	Regeneration
Repentance unto Life	Adoption
	Sanctification

The reasons for the above changes are obvious. Regeneration, or the New Birth, had always occupied a central place in the preaching of Cumberland Presbyterians, but had never been given the prominence in the Confession of Faith which it deserved. On the other hand, Cumberland Presbyterians had never believed in *Effectual* Calling (meaning that the call of God to the elect is irresistible), although the term still stood as a heading in the official creed of the church. As to the order of subjects, the order in the older Confession fit in well with a creed which based man's salvation entirely upon God's decree of election. If a man had no decision to make regarding his salvation, Faith and Repentance might as well come after Justification as before. Since Cumberland Presbyterians believe, however, that man has the responsibility of accepting or rejecting the gracious influence of the Holy Spirit, and since they believe the condition of Justification to be, not Effectual Calling, but Faith, it naturally follows that Repentance and Saving Faith precede Justification.

Simplification of Language and Style. The Westminster Confession was written in 1642. Since all living languages are constantly changing, the meaning of many words and phrases had changed in the course of two hundred forty years, and other phrases in vogue at the earlier date had ceased to be used or understood. Furhermore, the style of the Westminster Confession was diffuse and tedious, the sentences long and difficult to understand. The revisers of the Confession of Faith, by rewriting all the sections and putting them in simpler terms, shortened the Confession and Catechism by more than one-half.

As an illustration of what was achieved through the simplification of the language and style, a passage from Chapter XX, "Of Christian Liberty, and Liberty of Conscience," is here cited from the Confession of Faith of 1814 (which at this point is identical with the Westminster Confession):

> "The liberty which Christ hath purchased for believers under the gospel consists in their freedom from the guilt of sin, the condemning wrath of God, the curse of the moral law, and in their being delivered from this present evil world, bondage to Satan, and dominion of sin, from the evil of afflictions, the sting of death, the victory of the

grave, and everlasting damnation; as also in their free access to God, and their yielding obedience unto him, not out of slavish fear, but a child-like love, and a willing mind. All which were common also to believers under the law: but under the New Testament, the liberty of Christians is further enlarged in their freedom from the yoke of the ceremonial law, to which the Jewish Church was subjected; and in greater boldness of access to the throne of grace, and in fuller communications of the free Spirit of God, than believers under the law did ordinarily partake of." [3]

The corresponding section in the Cumberland Presbyterian Confession of Faith as adopted in 1883 reads as follows:

"The liberty that Christ has secured to believers under the gospel consists in freedom from the guilt and penal consequences of sin, in their free access to God, and in their yielding obedience to him, not from a slavish fear, but from a cheerful and confiding love." [4]

Elimination of Objectionable Statements. It was impossible to eliminate all objectionable statements from a Confession as self-consistent as the Westminster Confession simply by expunging a few sentences here and there and writing corrected statements in their places. Only by a complete rewriting of the whole was it possible to eliminate all traces of "limitarianism." This could never have been accomplished by piecemeal revision, footnotes, or explanatory statements.

THE STEWARDSHIP AMENDMENT

In 1955, a year in which emphasis was to be given to the biblical doctrine and practice of tithing, a proposed amendment to the Confession of Faith was submitted by Robert Donnell Presbytery setting forth the belief of the church in the practice of tithing. This amendment was passed by the General Assembly and submitted to the presbyteries for their approval, and it received the affirmative vote of the requisite three-fourths majority of the presbyteries.

The next General Assembly, however, expressed the desire that this doctrine should be set in its larger context under the head of "Christian Stewardship." A special committee was appointed to write an amendment which would carry out the wishes of the

Assembly. Such an amendment was submitted to the General Assembly in 1957 in the form of a section on "Christian Stewardship." Following its approval by the General Assembly and the requisite number of presbyteries, it became sections 79-84 of the Confession of Faith.

PIONEERS IN CREED REVISION

It has already been noted that the Cumberland Synod, in 1814, affirmed its right "to adopt what they think right, and expunge what they think erroneous, from any *human creed*." On this basis the synod proceeded to make a number of radical changes in the Confession which had been adopted as the Confession of Cumberland Presbytery in 1810. Furthermore, as more time elapsed, the need to bring the Confession of Faith more nearly in line with what was actually believed and taught by Cumberland Presbyterians became apparent. Again the Cumberland Presbyterian Church made the revisions it deemed proper, even though these revisions meant a virtual rewriting of the older Confession. Again in recent years, moved by the modern rediscovery of the biblical doctrine of Christian stewardship, Cumberland Presbyterians gave expression to their belief in that doctrine by giving it a place in their Confession of Faith.

The changing of a time-honored creedal statement is not easy, as is evident by the consistent refusal of the larger Presbyterian bodies to make any real change in the text of the Westminster Confession, even though there has been, at different times, agitation for revision.[5] From the time of the founding fathers, Cumberland Presbyterians have been willing to make changes in structure, methods, and program to meet new and changing situations. In like manner, there has been willingness to make changes in doctrinal statements when new experiences and a new understanding of biblical truth have led to the questioning of interpretations formerly held. There is a need with the passage of time to revise creedal statements, just as there is a need for new translations of the Holy Scriptures. Cumberland Presbyterians have been sensitive to that need.

SOMETHING TO THINK ABOUT

1. What was the first Confession of Faith used by Cumberland Presbyterians? Why was it soon necessary for them to formulate confessional statements of their own?

2. What were the principal changes made in the Confession of Faith adopted in 1814?

3. The committees appointed in 1881 to revise the Confession of Faith attempted to draw "with precision" the boundaries between the Cumberland Presbyterian theological scheme and those of other churches and sought to allow the utmost liberty of opinion within these bounds. This has resulted in some statements which are more vague or indefinite than some persons would desire. What would be the effect if these doctrines were defined in more detail? Is there value in not being explicit on some issues? Why?

4. Is the order of subjects as found in the revised Confession of Faith more in keeping with the plan of salvation as preached by Cumberland Presbyterians than was the order in the Confession of 1814? Why?

5. What is the difference between "Effectual Calling" and "Divine Influence"?

6. Why do you think a new chapter on "Regeneration" was included in the revised Confession of Faith?

7. Why was a chapter on "Christian Stewardship" inserted into the Confession of Faith in recent years?

8. Is it as necessary to revise church creeds periodically as it is to have new translations of the Scriptures? Why? What difference is there between revising a creed and revising or retranslating the Bible?

9. Why is it usually difficult to revise a creedal statement?

10. Attempts at Union

As HAS ALREADY been pointed out, the founders of the Cumberland Presbyterian Church did not intend to establish another denomination. They were seeking rather to secure for the ministers who would be ordained the freedom to accept the Presbyterian Confession of Faith with certain reservations as they themselves had done.

Our church founders hoped for a reunion with the Presbyterian Church. The "Circular Letter" sent out in 1810 by order of the Cumberland Presbytery stated "that we have it in view as a Presbytery to continue, or make another proposition to the Synod of Kentucky, or some other Synod, for a re-union, if we can obtain it without violating our natural and scriptural rights." In April, 1812, communications with reference to a possible reunion were sent to the presbyteries of Muhlenburg and West Tennessee of the Presbyterian Church. These overtures were rejected, however, and West Tennessee Presbytery went so far as to pass an order prohibiting the members of its churches from partaking of the Lord's Supper with Cumberland Presbyterians.

EFFORTS AT UNION, 1813 TO 1903

No further attempts at union appear to have been made until after the War Between the States, although the General Assembly which met in 1860, "seeing that the great Presbyterian family embrace alike the same church government, and that in their oral

121

addresses they are doctrinally converging to the same standpoint," ventured to "cherish the fond hope that the day is not far distant when the entire family shall be represented in one General Assembly."

In 1867, the General Assembly of the Cumberland Presbyterian Church took steps looking toward union with the Presbyterian Church, U. S., which occupied the southern states. This church had come into separate existence at the beginning of the War Between the States in consequence of resolutions adopted by the General Assembly of the Presbyterian Church, U. S. A. These resolutions virtually made loyalty to the United States a condition of church membership. In the attempt to formulate an acceptable basis for union, the committee of the Cumberland Presbyterian Church proposed to surrender the Cumberland name and to accept the standards of the Presbyterian Church, U. S., on the subject of ministerial education. It was proposed, however, either that the Confession of Faith and Catechism of the Cumberland Presbyterian Church be accepted by the united church, or that verbal changes be made in the Presbyterian Confession which would satisfactorily eliminate the idea of fatality. The attempt failed because the Presbyterian committee was unwilling to recommend such changes in its doctrinal standards.

The next attempt at union was with the Presbyterian Church, U. S. A., beginning in the year 1873. The committee of the Cumberland Presbyterian Church submitted, as a basis for union, a proposal that the Form of Government and Discipline of the Presbyterian Church, U. S. A., be adopted by the united church, but that both confessions of faith be retained as they were and regarded as of equal authority. It was proposed that in the licensure and ordination of ministers the individual be allowed to choose which of the two confessions he would accept. The Presbyterian committee, however, was unwilling to recommend union on this basis, and the negotiations were concluded without the submission of any plan to the two General Assemblies.

Beginning in 1881, negotiations were opened for union with the General Synod of the Evangelical Lutheran Church. The negotiations, which were carried on through correspondence, disclosed that while the Lutheran body favored a closer and more hearty fraternal union, they believed the difficulties in the way of organic union insurmountable. The Lutherans felt that unless unanimous consent on the part of all the churches of both denominations could be assured, the effect would be only to produce an additional number of factions. The committee of the Cumberland Presbyterian Church felt it unwise to press for positive action, at least not until the matter of the revision of their own Confession of Faith, then under consideration, should be settled.

In 1882, the Methodist Protestant Church, through its fraternal messenger to the Cumberland Presbyterian General Assembly, opened negotiations for a union of the two bodies. The Methodist Protestants had separated from the main body of Methodists in 1828 over their demand for lay representation in the conferences and had set up a Methodist church without bishops. A joint conference of the committees appointed to represent the two churches was held in the year 1886. It was found that no serious impediment to union existed in the government of the two churches, nor in their doctrines except on the question of the "preservation of believers." Since the Confession of Faith of the Cumberland Presbyterian Church was considered more full and systematic, it was recommended for favorable consideration as the creed of the united church with the suggestion that the question as to the certainty or uncertainty of the preservation of believers be left unexpressed. The General Assembly of the Cumberland Presbyterian Church in 1887 considered the report of this joint conference but expressed its "unwillingness to omit from our system of faith a doctrine so precious to us as that of the 'preservation of believers.' " The General Conference of the Methodist Protestant Church, meeting in 1888, took unfavorable action on the question of organic union, and so the negotiations were closed.

From the foregoing it will be seen that Cumberland Presbyterians at one time or another expressed their willingness to give up the name "Cumberland" and to accept the standards for ministerial education held by the larger Presbyterian bodies in order to achieve union. They were cautious, however, in matters of doctrine lest their "middle ground" theology, or at least the liberty

of their ministers, elders, deacons and members to hold and preach
that system of doctrine, be compromised.

ANOTHER UNION MOVEMENT INITIATED

In 1903, the General Assembly of the Cumberland Presbyterian Church, meeting in Nashville, Tennessee, had before it
memorials from nine presbyteries and two synods favoring some
sort of action looking to the union of the Cumberland Presbyterian
Church with the Presbyterian Church, U. S. A. There were also
memorials from ten presbyteries opposing such action. The result
of the consideration of these memorials was the appointment of a
Committee on Presbyterian Fraternity and Union "to confer with
such like Committees as may be appointed by other Presbyterian
bodies, in regard to the desirability and practicability of closer
affiliation and organic union among the members of the Presbyterian family in the United States."

Although the appointment of the committee contemplated
action looking to negotiations for the union of all Presbyterian
bodies, the efforts of the committee were confined to negotiations
with the Presbyterian Church, U. S. A. Since the withdrawal of the
southern presbyteries in 1861, this church had been principally
confined to the North and West. The General Assembly of the
Presbyterian Church, U. S. declined to appoint a committee to
confer on the subject of union.

THE PROPOSED PLAN OF UNION

During the ensuing year, the committees from the Cumberland
Presbyterian Church and the Presbyterian Church, U. S. A. held
three joint meetings. The result was the drafting of a Joint Report
on Union to be submitted to the General Assemblies of the two
churches in their 1904 meetings.

This report consisted of a "Plan of Reunion and Union of the
Two Churches" embodying four points, a series of eight "Concurrent Declarations," and three "Recommendations." The "Plan of
Reunion and Union" provided that the two churches be united
under the name of The Presbyterian Church in the United States
of America, and that the union be effected "on the doctrinal basis

of the Confession of Faith of the Presbyterian Church in the United States of America, as revised in 1903, and of its other doctrinal and ecclesiastical standards" and that "the Scriptures of the Old and New Testaments shall be acknowledged as the inspired word of God, the only infallible rule of faith and practice." It was further provided that each General Assembly should submit this basis of union to the presbyteries during the ensuing year for their approval or disapproval, and that, if the two General Assemblies should find the proposed basis of union to be approved by the constitutional majority, the union should then be binding.

One of the Concurrent Declarations stated that "it is mutually recognized that such agreement now exists between the systems of doctrine contained in the Confession of Faith of the two Churches as to warrant this union—a union honoring alike to both." All ministers and churches in the two denominations were to have the same standing in the united church as they had in their respective connections at the consummation of the union.

It was recommended that a change be made in the Form of Government of the Presbyterian Church, U. S. A. to "allow additional or separate Presbyteries and Synods to be organized in exceptional cases, wholly or in part, within the territorial bounds of existing Presbyteries or Synods respectively, for a particular race or nationality, if desired by such race or nationality."

The joint report was signed by all members of the committee from the Cumberland Presbyterian Church, but two members of the committee from the Presbyterian Church, U. S. A., registered their dissent. Although the initiative had been taken by persons within the Cumberland Presbyterian Church who desired union with the larger Presbyterian body, the Presbyterian Church, U. S. A. welcomed the union as a means by which its work might be extended into the South and the Southwest.

DID REVISION REVISE?

It has been noted that the plan of union was to be effected on the doctrinal basis of "The Confession of Faith of the Presbyterian Church in the United States of America, as revised in 1903, and of its other doctrinal and ecclesiastical standards." What was the nature of this revision? It consisted of (1) a Declaratory Statement intended to interpret Chapter III and Chapter X, Section 3; (2) slight changes in the wording of three other sections (which, however, had to do with matters which were never called in question by Cumberland Presbyterians); and (3) the addition of two chapters on "the Holy Spirit" and "the Love of God and Missions." The Declaratory Statement reads as follows:

> "While the ordination vow of ministers, ruling elders, and deacons as set forth in the Form of Government, requires the reception and adoption of the Confession of Faith only as containing the System of Doctrine taught in the Holy Scriptures, nevertheless, seeing that the desire has been formally expressed for a disavowal by the Church of certain inferences drawn from statements in the Confession of Faith, and also for a declaration of certain aspects of revealed truth which appear at the present time to call for more explicit statement, therefore the Presbyerian Church in the United States of America does authoritatively declare as follows:
>
> "First, With reference to Chapter III. of the Confession of Faith: that concerning those who are saved in Christ, the doctrine of God's eternal decree is held in harmony with the doctrine of His love to all mankind, His gift of His Son to be the propitiation for the sins of the whole world, and His readiness to bestow His saving grace on all who seek it. That concerning those who perish, the doctrine of God's eternal decree is held in harmony with the doctrine that God desires not the death of any sinner, but has provided in Christ a salvation sufficient for all, adapted to all, and freely offered in the Gospel to all; that men are fully responsible for their treatment of God's gracious offer; that His decree hinders no man from accepting that offer; and that no man is condemned except on the ground of his sin.
>
> "Second, With reference to Chapter X., Section 3, of the Confession of Faith, that it is not to be regarded as teaching that any who die in infancy are lost. We believe that all dying in infancy are included in the election of grace, and are regenerated and saved by Christ through the Spirit, who works when and where and how He pleases." [1]

It should be noted that the Declaratory Statement dealt only with one chapter and one section of another chapter of the Confession of Faith although the doctrine of unconditional election and reprobation is present either explicitly or implicitly in no less than thirteen chapters. No change was made in the text of the sections the Declaratory Statement was designed to interpret. Although the Declaratory Statement asserts that the doctrine of God's decrees as set forth in Chapter III is to be held in harmony with His love to all mankind (and kindred doctrines), no indication is given as to how the two can be harmonized.

The members of the Cumberland Presbyterian Committee on Fraternity and Union, in their report to the General Assembly in 1904, argued at length that "revision has revised." At the same time, the committee of the Presbyterian Church, U. S. A. was saying to its General Assembly:

> "It was made clear to the brethren of the Committee on Fraternity and Union of the Cumberland Presbyterian Church, at the outset of our conferences, that the Revision of the Confession of Faith recently undertaken by our Church was not occasioned by any pressure from without, but was purely a movement within our own denomination. It was also stated that the purposes of the movement were two: to disavow inferences drawn from certain statements in the Confession of Faith, and also to set forth clearly some aspects of revealed truth which appeared to call for more explicit statement. In addition it was declared that the effect of the adoption of the Declaratory Statement as a part of the Constitution, was simply to give legal standing to interpretations of Chapter iii and of Chapter x, Section 3, which previously had seemed to have merely the force of private opinion, *and that the revision of the Confession of Faith had effected no material change in the doctrinal attitude of our Church"* [2] (italics ours).

THE VOTE ON THE PLAN OF UNION

The Cumberland Presbyterian General Assembly met in 1904 at Dallas, Texas, and the Joint Report on Union was before the Assembly. After a lengthy discussion which covered the great part of two days, the proposal to submit the proposed basis of union to the presbyteries "in the usual constitutional manner" was carried on Wednesday night, May 25, by a vote of 162 to 74, four votes more than the two-thirds majority required by the Constitution. A total of 251 commissioners were enrolled, which means that fifteen commissioners were absent when the vote was taken.

During the ensuing year the presbyteries voted on the proposal. When the votes were canvassed at Fresno, California, in 1905, it was found that sixty presbyteries had voted for approval of the union and fifty-one had voted their disapproval. Two presbyteries did not report, and one voted for union conditionally. At that time only a simple majority of presbyteries was required to effect a constitutional change, each presbytery voting as a unit. Since there were one hundred and fourteen presbyteries, an affirmative vote of fifty-eight presbyteries was required to carry the proposal. Two more than that number had voted their approval. The summary of the vote within the presbyteries showed that 691 ministers and 649 ruling elders had voted for the union, making a total affirmative vote of 1,340, while 470 ministers and 1,007 ruling elders, or a total of 1,477, had voted against union. There were 137 more votes cast against union than were cast for union, but the votes were so distributed that a majority of presbyteries voted for union. The recommendation of the majority of the Special Committee on Organic Union, that the General Assembly declare the union "constitutionally agreed to by the Cumberland Presbyterian Church," was adopted by a vote of 137 to 110.

Meanwhile, in the Presbyterian Church, U. S. A., 194 of its 241 presbyteries had voted for the union. This was well over the two-thirds vote of the presbyteries required by that denomination.

THE DECATUR ASSEMBLY

Details of carrying the union into effect having been left to the committees of the two churches, the plan for accomplishing this task was embodied in the "Joint Report on Reunion and Union" which was submitted to the Cumberland Presbyterian General Assembly meeting at Decatur, Illinois, May 17-24, 1906. This joint report was adopted by the General Assembly by a vote of 165 to 91. This report called for adjournment of the Cumberland Presbyterian General Assembly *sine die* as a separate Assembly to meet in and as a part of the General Assembly of the Presbyterian

Church, U. S. A., in 1907. Prior to adjournment, one hundred commissioners, led by Ruling Elder Joe H. Fussell, entered a protest against the carrying into effect of the provisions of this report. The third point in this protest reads as follows:

> "3. Said Assembly had no power to transfer the allegiance of the ministers, elders, deacons, officers, particular churches, judicatories, boards, and committees to another denomination of Christians, and make them amenable to another church creed and constitution." [3]

There had been much opposition to the proposed union within the Cumberland Presbyterian Church, as indicated by the number of memorials against union when the idea was initiated in 1903, the bare constitutional majorities the proponents of union were able to muster, and the number of commissioners protesting against the actions of the General Assemblies of 1905 and 1906. Under these conditions it could hardly be expected that the union would meet with general acceptance. Now that the vote had been taken, some of those who had opposed the plan of union, as well as those who had favored it, believed that all Cumberland Presbyterians were obligated to go along with the union. Had not the ministers, ruling elders, and deacons taken the vow to submit themselves to their brethren in the Lord assembled in the various church courts and "to study the peace of the Church"? Others, however, could not with a good conscience acquiesce in an action which meant the surrender of their Confession of Faith and the acceptance of the Confession of Faith of the Presbyterian Church in the U. S. A. In their ordination they had adopted the Confession of Faith of the Cumberland Presbyterian Church, and no man or group of men, they contended, had the right or power to transfer their allegiance to a church which held to a different Confession of Faith. Thus it was apparent that searchings of heart, differences in point of view, and division within the Cumberland Presbyterian forces would follow the attempted consummation of the union.

On May 24, 1906, over the protest of the one hundred commissioners already mentioned, the General Assembly of the Cumberland Presbyterian Church voted to adjourn *sine die* according to the decision previously reached. At this point Ruling Elder Joe H. Fussell announced that the meetings of the General Assembly would be continued in the Hall of the Grand Army of the Republic, inasmuch as use of the church building had been denied them for this purpose. In this continued session of the General Assembly, one hundred and six commissioners were enrolled. The General Assembly elected the Reverend J. L. Hudgins moderator and then proceeded to fill vacancies in its offices, boards, and committees and to attend to other routine business, after which it adjourned to meet in May, 1907, at the birthplace of the Cumberland Presbyterian Church in Dickson County, Tennessee.

SOMETHING TO THINK ABOUT

1. What efforts were made by Cumberland Presbyterians toward union with other church bodies prior to 1903? Why were these efforts unsuccessful?

2. What were the terms of union proposed by the joint committee on union of the Cumberland Presbyterian Church and the Presbyterian Church, U. S. A., in 1904?

3. Did the revision made in 1903 by the Presbyterian Church, U. S. A. really change those doctrinal statements to which the founders of the Cumberland Presbyterian Church took exception? Give reasons for your answer.

4. What did the vote on the Plan of Union by the presbyteries indicate as to the attitude of the Cumberland Presbyterian Church as a whole toward the proposed union?

5. Is it ever advisable to bring about church union on terms which are unacceptable to a large segment of either church? Why?

6. Why did the 106 commissioners at the General Assembly in 1906 resolve to perpetuate the Cumberland Presbyterian Church? Were they justified in this action? Give reasons for your answer.

11. Reconstruction and Advance

DURING THE SUMMER and fall of 1906 the various presbyteries met. Inevitably the question would arise, "Is this a presbytery of the Cumberland Presbyterian Church or a presbytery of the Presbyterian Church, U. S. A.?" Then came the painful ordeal of division as one or the other group prevailed and the minority walked out to form a presbytery according to its convictions regarding the union.

THE TASK OF REORGANIZATION

The Minutes of the Cumberland Presbyterian General Assembly for 1907 list eighty presbyteries. Three of these did not have a quorum of ministers, and thirty-two had fewer than six ordained ministers. Thirty presbyteries were reported as being in a disorganized condition. Two of these were later reorganized. Seventy-four presbyteries were represented in the Cumberland Presbyterian General Assembly in 1907. There were no commissioners to the Cumberland Presbyterian General Assembly after 1906 from any presbyteries in the synods of Kansas, Ohio, Oregon, or Pennsylvania.

Since in many instances a majority of the remaining ministers were aged, further consolidation of presbyteries soon became necessary. Of the three presbyteries in the state of Iowa, only one small presbytery remained. It was attached to the Synod of Missouri, and in 1919 its members were added to McGee Presbytery. The three presbyteries which formerly had composed the Synod of Indiana were consolidated in 1910 to form one presbytery which was attached to Illinois Synod. By 1914, the twenty presbyteries in the state of Texas had been reduced to eleven. In the state of Missouri eight presbyteries remained where there had been thirteen. In the state of Illinois the number of presbyteries had been reduced from ten to five. Three small presbyteries remained in the Synod of Mississippi, where there had been five. Only in the Synods of Alabama, Tennessee, and West Tennessee did all the presbyteries remain intact.

On the other hand, two new synods were formed after the attempted union. In 1915 the Synod of West Texas and New Mexico was created. It was composed of the presbyteries of Amarillo, Brownwood, Roswell, and Sweetwater. This synod which was from the beginning numerically weak was further weakened by the coming of World War I and two years of drouth. It held only four meetings. By action of the General Assembly in 1920 its presbyteries were again attached to Texas Synod. In 1925 provision was made for the organization of East Tennessee Synod composed of the presbyteries of Chattanooga, East Tennessee, and Knoxville. This synod held its first meeting in Knoxville in November, 1926. It continues to be an effective judicatory.

The work of reorganization was also going on at the local level as those who chose to remain Cumberland Presbyterians sought to preserve existing churches or their ministers sought to gather the remnants that remained when churches were absorbed into the Presbyterian Church, U. S. A. In some local churches there was virtual unanimity either for or against the union, but in many there was division.

The final outcome on the local level was complicated by the numerous lawsuits which were filed for the possession of church property. In Tennessee the unionists went farther in their litigation than to deal simply with property interests. An injunction was filed by and in the name of certain former Cumberland Presbyterians "and all other ministers, officers, and members of the Presbyterian Church in the U. S. A." to restrain and prohibit Cumberland Presbyterians (1) from interfering with the unionists' exclusive possession of property which belonged to the Cumberland Presbyterian Church, (2) from asserting any right thereto in any court of law or equity, (3) from the use of the name of the Cumberland Presbyterian Church, and (4) from using the Confession of Faith of the Cumberland Presbyterian Church. The lawsuits which followed produced tension and bitterness on both sides. Except in the state of Tennessee, where the decision was favorable to the Cumberland Presbyterians, the courts generally refused to go behind the decision of the General Assembly and therefore upheld the union.

The records for 1907 list 570 ordained ministers, 54 licentiates, and 64 candidates for the ministry as compared with 1,514 ordained ministers, 121 licentiates, and 175 candidates listed in 1906. It is difficult to determine the number of churches which remained Cumberland Presbyterian, for all churches which had been listed in 1906 were carried on the rolls of many presbyteries pending the outcome of the litigation. The records for 1906 list 2,869 churches with a total membership of 185,212. The records for 1921 list 1,312 churches and give the total membership as 64,452.

Except in the state of Tennessee where much of the local church property was retained by the Cumberland Presbyterians, most of the town and city churches were lost to the Presbyterian Church, U. S. A. Notable exceptions were Jefferson Avenue, Evansville, Indiana, and Marshall, Texas (where the congregation paid a sum of money to obtain a quitclaim to its property from the Presbyterian Church, U. S. A.). In Memphis, Tennessee, the property of the largest church, Court Avenue, was awarded to the Presbyterian Church, U. S. A. Numerous former Cumberland Presbyterian congregations continue today as United Presbyterian churches. For example, the Court Avenue church in Memphis, after a union with an Associate Reformed Presbyterian congregation, is now known as Lindsay Memorial Church.

Re-establishment of churches in the cities was a difficult task because of the costs involved in purchasing property and erecting new buildings. As is pointed out frequently in the annual reports of the Board of Missions for the years following 1906, many churches which previously had given strong support to the Cumberland Presbyterian Church were now themselves in need of help. Financial support of the sort needed for establishing churches in the urban areas was virtually non-existent. The problem of securing ministerial leadership presented another difficulty, for a disproportionate number of the ministers who remained in the Cumberland Presbyterian Church had passed the age for active service as pastors. In a number of towns and cities there remained respectable congregations of those who could not see their way clear to go into the union; but not infrequently these were eventually disbanded because of lack of competent ministerial leadership. Thus the Cumberland Presbyterian Church again became largely a rural church.

Efforts were made to re-establish churches in some of the cities where Cumberland Presbyterian churches had formerly existed, and with some degree of success. Central Church, of Memphis, starting with seven members, experienced a substantial growth and became the parent church for all the Cumberland Presbyterian churches now in existence in the Memphis metropolitan area. At Austin, Texas, the old Cumberland Presbyterian church building which the Presbyterians had sold to a Baptist church was purchased in 1914 for $23,000 by the Cumberland Presbyterians and a church re-established. A substantial church was established in Birmingham, Alabama. Churches were also re-organized in Dallas and Fort Worth, Texas; Fresno and Los Angeles, California; Muskogee, Oklahoma; Warrensburg, Marshall Moberly, Sedalia, and Springfield, Missouri; Paducah, Owensboro, and Princeton, Kentucky; and other points. Some support was given for several years to a church at Merced, California, and efforts were made to re-establish churches at Pueblo and Colorado Springs, Colorado, but these efforts did not result in the establishment of permanent churches.

The whole story of the period of reconstruction cannot be told here. It is a story of sacrificial service rendered by men who counted faithfulness to their convictions more important than material gain. At the risk of omitting many important developments, attention will be given to several decisions which, in retrospect, seem to have influenced significantly the development of the Cumberland Presbyterian Church.

THE DECISION TO ENDOW AN
INSTITUTION OF LEARNING

In 1906, all schools, publishing interests, and benevolent institutions were taken into the Presbyterian Church in the U. S. A. with the exception of Bethel College, McKenzie, Tennessee, which was finally awarded to the Cumberland Presbyterian Church. In 1908, the General Assembly's Board of Education made arrangements with the trustees of Bethel College to open a theological school in a room at Bethel College and employed the Reverend P. F. Johnson as dean and sole professor. In 1913, as the result of a compromise settlement with Cumberland University, the Cumberland Presbyterian Church received the net amount of $33,750, which was set apart as endowment for a theological school. With the income from this fund a second professor, the Reverend S. H. Braly, was employed. The General Assembly then resolved to raise $100,000 to endow a theological school.

On February 20, 1918, a conference of some thirty-four interested persons met in Memphis, Tennessee, to consider the educational needs of the denomination. The conference submitted to the General Assembly proposals asking that the Assembly establish and maintain one educational institution which should include both literary and theological departments, and that provision be made for the raising of one-half million dollars as endowment for the literary department. This plan was not to interfere with the plan already in progress for raising the theological endowment. The plan proposed by the conference was adopted substantially as submitted.

The next year the two endowment campaigns were merged into one campaign for $500,000, with the provision that the theological department should receive one-fifth of the amount raised until its quota of $100,000 endowment should be reached.

By 1922 the General Assembly was ready to decide where its one school should be located. In the meantime, the Synod of West Tennessee had given Bethel College to the General Assembly.

Nashville, Memphis, Jackson, and McKenzie, Tennessee, each submitted proposals to secure the location of the school. The General
Assembly's vote was in favor of McKenzie. The town gave $75,000
and added some acreage to the existing campus of Bethel College.

It was decided that Bethel College would be merged into the
new school and that, for the present, the school would bear the
name of Bethel College. This decision has never been changed. The
same General Assembly made provision for the consolidation of
the Board of Education, Board of Trustees of Bethel College, and
Board of Trustees of the Theological Seminary to form one board
to be known as the Cumberland Presbyterian Board of Education.
A new administration building was erected with the money given
by McKenzie, and the school opened under a new administration in
the fall of 1923.

A DENOMINATIONAL BUDGET ESTABLISHED

For many years each board of the General Assembly had
made its own appeal for support from the church, certain months
of the year being designated for the appeal of each board. Growing
out of a conference of representatives of the various boards, held at
Clarksville, Tennessee, in December, 1918, the General Assembly
in 1919 set a goal of $90,000 for support of the work of the
Assembly boards for the ensuing year, adopted a percentage basis
for the distribution of the funds, and appointed an executive committee to direct the campaign and a treasurer to receive and dis-
burse the funds. The Woman's Board of Missions, which had the
oversight of the work of foreign missions, was not included. Thus
began what came to be known as the denominational budget.
Although receipts the first year, and for many years thereafter,
fell far short of the suggested goal, this plan proved to be a more
effective way of providing operating funds for the work of the
various boards and agencies of the General Assembly.

A BOARD OF YOUNG PEOPLE'S WORK CREATED

For some years prior to 1927, the young people's work of the
denomination was under the supervision of the Board of Publication, Sunday School, and Young People's Work. This board also

had the oversight of the publishing house—production and publication of Sunday school literature and *The Cumberland Presbyterian,* the weekly church paper. In 1927, in response to a memorial from Indiana Presbytery and the supporting pleas of other interested persons, the General Assembly separated the young people's work from this board and created a Board of Young People's Work. It was believed that the work of the young people would advance faster under a separate board. Shortly thereafter, the Board of Young People's Work employed the Reverend Clark Williamson as General Secretary of Young People's Work. It was under his supervision that the presbyterial and synodic youth organizations, the camping program, and the program of leadership education took form.

The Young People's General Assembly (YPGA), which had been organized in 1924, was transformed into a leadership education school with courses of study in Bible, Cumberland Presbyterian doctrine, and personal spiritual nurture, and with leadership development being offered and standard credits issued. The existing synodic camps, along with those that subsequently came into being, were planned according to the same pattern. By 1935, 4,272 credit certificates had been issued to 2,400 individuals. During the year 1934, 1,201 credit certificates were issued for courses of study completed in YPGA, nine synodic camps, five presbyterial camps, and twenty-four local leadership schools and classes. By 1942, the ten synods and twenty-six presbyteries had promoted camps.

The values of the leadership education program, as carried on largely through YPGA and synodic and presbyterial camps, consisted not only in the actual knowledge gained but in a better understanding of the total mission and work of the church. Many of the ministers now serving in the Cumberland Presbyterian Church answered the call to the work of the ministry while in camp.

In 1936, largely as a result of the fact that the Board of Publication and Sunday School Work had adopted a program of leadership education similar to that being promoted by the Board of Young People's Work, the General Assembly created the Board of Christian Education to take over all the responsibilities of the Board of Young People's Work plus that part of the work of the

Board of Publication and Sunday School Work which pertained to "organization, promotion of Sunday schools and their work, setting up standards and forming curriculum for training Sunday school teachers and workers, and the supervision of the work of Sunday schools throughout the denomination." Youth work became a department within the Board of Christian Education. While the production and publication of Sunday school literature remained under the supervision of the Board of Publication and Sunday School Work, the influence of the Board of Christian Education upon the type of materials offered was increasingly felt.

THE GENERAL ASSEMBLY'S BOARDS AND AGENCIES ARE REORGANIZED

In the spring of 1948, the moderator of the General Assembly, the Reverend Morris Pepper, called a conference on the policy and program of the church to which all interested persons were invited. About 160 persons attended this conference which was held at the Central Cumberland Presbyterian Church, Memphis, Tennessee, April 6 and 7. The moderator presented to the conference a paper outlining his views concerning the state of the church and the direction that should be taken. Those recommendations with which the conference as a whole was found to be in agreement were embodied in the moderator's report to the General Assembly which met in Nashville, Tennessee, in June, 1948.

As a result of the moderator's recommendations, the Board of Publication and Sunday School Work and the Board of Christian Education were consolidated to form the Board of Publication and Christian Education. The functions of the Educational Endowment Commission, the Board of Trustees of the General Assembly, the Board of Tithing and Budget, and the Board of Ministerial Relief (with the exception of the operation of the Cumberland Presbyterian Children's Home, at Denton, Texas) were vested in a single board to be known as the Board of Finance. Provision was made for a Board of Trustees of the Children's Home. The name of the Board of Missions and Church Erection was changed to the Board of Missions and Evangelism. The Board of Foreign Missions and the Cumberland Presbyterian Board of Education were to continue functioning as heretofore except that all endowment funds of these agencies were to be administered by the Board of Finance.

THE PROGRAM OF ACHIEVEMENT IS LAUNCHED

The Board of Finance, in its report to the General Assembly which met in Muskogee, Oklahoma, in June, 1949, recommended the launching of the Program of Achievement, a financial campaign in the amount of $350,000. It would provide $100,000 additional endowment for Bethel College, $100,000 for the erection of a building to house the Bethel College Library and the Theological Seminary, and $150,000 to build a Denominational Center in Memphis, Tennessee. Previously the decision had been made to sell the publishing house in Nashville and to erect a new building to house the publishing interests and the offices of boards of the General Assembly.

By the time the Board of Finance made its report to the General Assembly in 1950, a total of $198,615.56 had been raised toward the Program of Achievement. Authorization was given for the erection of the two buildings—the Denominational Center at Memphis, and the Library-Seminary Building on the Bethel College campus in McKenzie. It was decided that the campaign would be continued until December 31, 1950.

By the time of the 1951 General Assembly, the receipts for the Program of Achievement had reached $266,041.52. Since the proportion allotted to Bethel College Endowment had already been sufficient to complete the original goal of $500,000 which had been set in 1918, it was decided that future receipts for the Program of Achievement would be allotted to the two building programs: two-fifths to retire indebtedness on the Library-Seminary Building, and three-fifths to retire the debt on the Denominational Center.

The erection of the two buildings mentioned above served a useful purpose. The housing of the offices of four of the General Assembly's boards and the stated clerk's office in the Denominational Center made possible better communication among the various agencies of the General Assembly and thus closer correlation of the work of these agencies. The Library-Seminary Building helped to clarify the identity of the theological seminary as well as to provide more adequate quarters for the Bethel College Library.

One of the greatest values of the Program of Achievement, however, was found in the fact that many Cumberland Presbyterian churches came to realize that they could contribute substantial sums of money to denominational causes. Many churches, both large and small, experienced a sense of achievement such as had not been felt for many years.

NEW CHURCHES ESTABLISHED AT HOME
AND ABROAD

The unified denominational budget brought more money into the treasury of the Board of Missions and Church Erection than it had been receiving. Thus during the 1920's this board was able to expend substantial amounts in the establishment of several new churches. Among the churches organized during the 1920's, which have since developed into self-supporting churches, are First Church, San Antonio, Texas; First Church, Kansas City, Missouri; West End Church, Birmingham, Alabama; Alabama City, Alabama (now the Forrest Avenue Church, of Gadsden); Tampa, Florida (now Lewis Memorial); Second (now Grace) and East Side, Memphis, Tennessee.

During the 1930's, despite the depression, a considerable amount of mission work continued. Acting upon a request from a group of Cumberland Presbyterians living in Detroit, Michigan, the General Assembly in 1929 had recommended that the Board of Missions and Church Erection take steps to establish a Cumberland Presbyterian Church in Detroit. This church was organized early in 1930. Other churches organized duing the 1930's, which developed into self-sustaining churches, included Denton, Texas; Rose City, North Little Rock, Arkansas; Longview, Texas; Shreveport, Louisiana; Park Avenue and Fifth (now Highland Heights), Memphis, Tennessee. There were also several attempts to establish churches which did not result in permanent congregations. During the depression years, the assistance that could be given new churches was meager.

Beginning about 1936, a missionary was employed in an

effort to re-establish the Cumberland Presbyterian Church in Ohio. Although several small congregations were organized, the only active churches which have survived are Avalon and Mayfield, both in Middletown, Ohio.

During the 1940's, churches were organized at Booneville, Pine Bluff, and Fort Smith, Arkansas; Lexington, Waverly, and Parsons, Tennessee; Louisville, Kentucky; Indianapolis, Indiana; Grace Church, Detroit, Michigan; Houston, Texas; and Cherokee, Alabama. During this period, a third attempt to establish a church in Huntsville, Alabama, was successful.

Attention has already been given, in chapter 6, to the foreign mission work which was attempted during this period. It should be noted again here that the Cumberland Presbyterian Church carried on mission work in South China and in Colombia, South America, and, near the end of the period, re-entered Japan. The mission work in these areas was well administered and enjoyed the benefit of good leadership. As has already been noted, foreign mission work during this period was largely supported by the women of the church working through local, presbyterial, and synodic auxiliaries and through the Woman's Board of Missions.

Despite many limitations in terms of organization, personnel, and financial resources, the leaders of the Cumberland Presbyterian Church were not merely waging a battle for survival, although the necessities of the times required that such a struggle be made if the Cumberland Presbyterian Church were to be maintained as an instrument for the spread of the gospel. They were doing the work of the church to the best of their understanding and abilities. They were preaching the gospel of Christ, often very effectively, to those who needed it, and they were interested in establishing churches in places where churches were needed. Although it was not until after 1930 that the church began to show a steady numerical growth, foundations were being laid for greater progress in the years to come.

SOMETHING TO THINK ABOUT

1. What had to be done by way of reorganizing and re-grouping following the attempted union of 1906?

2. Why was the Cumberland Presbyterian Church slow in re-establishing city churches following the attempted union?

3. Why was it deemed necessary to raise $500,000 to endow a college?

4. What advantages are there in having one denominational budget for financing the enterprises of the church rather than having each board and agency make its own appeal? Are there disadvantages?

5. What values have come from the summer camp program of the Cumberland Presbyterian Church?

6. In what respects was the structure of the boards of the General Assembly simplified by the reorganization which took place in 1948?

7. What values were derived from the Program of Achievement?

8. What is the present membership of the churches listed as having been organized during the period 1920-1950? What did these churches contribute to Our United Outreach last year? (See the latest *Yearbook of the General Assembly*.)

9. What has been the progress of your congregation since 1930? How has your congregation participated in the mission of the church in your community? beyond your community?

12. A Decade of Progress

AFTER GOING THROUGH a period of reorganization, the Cumberland Presbyterian Church in 1950 found itself face to face with new frontiers, for again there was a great movement of population. People had been moving to the cities for many years, but the process was accelerated during World War II when many persons accepted employment in defense plants. Decreased acreage allotments for money crops forced people off the farms, so that, in many areas, rural communities became all but depopulated. If the church was to go where the people were going, churches had to be built in urban areas.

MISSIONARY OUTREACH

During the early part of the decade, several significant actions were taken by the Board of Missions and Evangelism. The first had to do with strengthening ministerial leadership in the rural areas where many churches were being served by ministers who were without college and seminary training. In its budget for 1951, the board included $10,000 for short-term in-service training schools for rural ministers who had not had the opportunity to obtain a college and seminary education. The funds were set up to provide instruction at the schools and scholarships for the ministers attending. Fifteen ministers attended the first school, which was held in the late summer of 1951. In 1957, attendance at the in-service school reached an all-time high of forty ministers. All the schools have been held on the campus of Bethel College, and since 1959 the seminary has shared in the financial support of the school by providing the cost of instruction. Although the Board of Missions and Evangelism still assumes the responsibility of providing scholarships for the men attending, various presbyteries are contributing scholarships, thus sharing in the enterprise. The ministry of many rural pastors has been rendered more effective through their attendance at the in-service school.

In 1951, the Reverend Raymond Kinslow was employed as a full-time worker for Choctaw Presbytery. The Choctaw Indians in southeastern Oklahoma were being seriously affected by the social change going on around them, and the need for providing a program suitable to the needs of the rising generation was widely felt. Within the next five years, four new churches were organized in Choctaw Presbytery, two of which were composed of white people. In June, 1953, the Reverend John Lovelace was sent to Choctaw Presbytery to serve as pastor of the newly organized churches at Honey Grove and Wright City. In 1955, Raymond Kinslow resigned as a missionary to Choctaw Presbytery. John Lovelace continued in this field, serving the Honey Grove and Oak Hill churches and giving general supervision to the Indian work, until early in 1959 when he and his family left Choctaw Presbytery to prepare to be missionaries in Colombia, South America. On July 1, 1959, the Reverend Charles Faith became a missionary to Choctaw Presbytery. During 1957 a manse had been built for the missionary in Idabel, Oklahoma. Material assistance to this project was given through vacation church school offerings and offerings contributed earlier by the young people of the Cumberland Presbyterian Church. In 1965, Charles Faith returned to the pastorate and Licentiate Claude Gilbert became missionary to Choctaw Presbytery.

The board's report to the General Assembly in 1952 announced the initiation of a new policy by which missionaries were to be employed and commissioned. These missionaries would be assigned to projects which involved the establishing of new churches. It was intended that, once the project to which the missionary was originally assigned had been established, he would be assigned to a new project in another locality. The board was still assisting several already existing churches under its previous policy of supplementing the salaries of pastors of churches which were accepted as mission projects, and naturally this phase of its work had to be continued for a while. During 1951, financial assistance had been given to ten urban projects: Madison, Tennessee; Moberly, Missouri; Fort Smith and Harrison, Arkansas; Houston and Corsicana, Texas; Florence, Alabama; Central City, Kentucky; and Clinton and Oklahoma City, Oklahoma.

Oklahoma City was opened as a mission project in December, 1951, and was the first project attempted under the new policy. The Reverend Paul F. Brown was the missionary. In 1952, the Reverend Virgil Weeks was sent as a missionary to Jackson, Mississippi. In its 1953 report, the board stated that churches had been organized at Jackson, Mississippi, and Oklahoma City, and approval had been given for opening projects in Oak Ridge, Tennessee, and the Meadowbrook subdivision of Fort Worth, Texas. The Reverend J. P. Bright was employed as the missionary at Oak Ridge, and the Reverend H. O. Bennett at Meadowbrook. The Meadowbrook Church was organized in May, 1953, and the church at Oak Ridge in February, 1954. In December, 1954, the Reverend Sidney Slaton was sent as the missionary to Wichita, Kansas, and the Reverend Dudley Condron to Tulsa, Oklahoma. Cumberland Presbyterian Sunday schools had been begun in these two cities several months earlier. The church at Wichita was organized March 20, 1955, and the church at Tulsa, August 28, 1955.

Meanwhile, various presbyteries and synods were initiating mission projects. The presbyterial boards of missions of Hopewell and Obion Presbyteries co-operated in establishing a church at Humboldt, Tennessee. This church was organized in May, 1953, and included the membership of Pleasant Hill, a near-by rural congregation which disbanded in order to be part of the new group. Memphis Presbytery initiated the organization of a church in the Colonial Acres subdivision of Memphis. Platte-Lexington Presbytery purchased property and erected a building in Raytown, Missouri, in the Kansas City area, and a missionary was assigned to this field in October, 1955. Crestline Church, in Birmingham, Alabama, was organized in December, 1964. This project was initiated by the Oak Grove congregation and established with the cooperation of Birmingham Presbytery and Alabama-Mississippi Synod. The project which resulted in the organization of the Modern Manor Church in Lubbock, Texas, which also was organized in 1954, was initiated by the First Cumberland Presbyterian Church of Lubbock and given support by Lubbock Presbytery. Lubbock Presbytery also arranged for the organization of a new church at Odessa, Texas. A church was organized at Tuscaloosa, Alabama, in March, 1955, under the sponsorship of New Hope and Birmingham Presbyteries, Alabama-Mississippi Synod, and the General Assembly's Board. In July, 1955, the Faith Church, St. Clair Shores, Michigan, was organized. This work was principally supported by Illinois Synod.

As early as 1957, the General Assembly's board authorized its executive secretary to seek to establish synodical, presbyterial, and local boards of missions and evangelism through which the denominational board might work by giving instruction and guidance and all help possible. These boards would be encouraged to develop their own leadership, seek out prospective mission points, establish a presbyterial or synodical budget for missions, and work under supervision of the General Assembly's board in the further development of the work. The following year the General Assembly's board announced that its policy would be to provide financial help for mission projects in "fringe" areas, while presbyteries and synods that were able to do so would be expected to provide the major financial support for mission projects in their bounds.

During the latter half of the decade, a number of mission projects were begun by presbyterial and synodic boards of missions, and in most cases the counsel and supervision of the General Assembly's board were sought. Among such projects were El Dorado, Arkansas, sponsored by Arkansas Synod; Tanglewood Church, Tyler, Texas, sponsored by McAdow Presbytery; Albuquerque, New Mexico, sponsored by Lubbock Presbytery; Sheffield, Alabama, sponsored by McGready Presbytery and Alabama-Mississippi Synod; Fairview, Columbus, Mississippi, sponsored by

New Hope Presbytery and Alabama-Mississippi Synod; Mayfield, Kentucky, sponsored by Mayfield Presbytery; Glasgow, Kentucky, sponsored by Cumberland Presbytery and Kentucky Synod; St. Luke and Donelson, sponsored by Nashville Presbytery; and Tullahoma, Tennessee, sponsored by Elk Presbytery with some assistance from Tennessee Synod. In some cases financial aid was eventually given by the General Assembly's board, while others were supported entirely by the sponsoring presbytery or synod.

The work of the General Assembly's board was not confined to urban projects. The Antioch church in Hill County, Texas, moved into Hillsboro in 1956 and became the hub for the formation of the Hill County Parish. A church begun in Livingston, Tennessee, under the direction of Cookeville Presbytery, along with two rural churches, became a part of the Dale Hollow Larger Parish. Both of these projects were aided financially by the General Assembly's board.

Altogether, fifty-three new churches appeared on the rolls of the various presbyteries during the decade of 1950-1960. At the end of the decade there were fellowships at Tullahoma, Tennessee; Mayfield, Kentucky; and Frayser and Whitehaven, in the Memphis, Tennessee, metropolitan area, which were on their way to becoming churches. During the decade there was a net increase in the Cumberland Presbyterian Church of 7,913 active members, 6,999 in the total reported membership, and 13,819 in Sunday school enrollment. The total amounts paid to pastors and expended for building and repairs virtually doubled. Despite the number of new churches organized, however, the total number of churches decreased from 1,035 to 984. In part, this reflected population changes which made the demise of some churches almost inevitable. In other instances, it reflected a failure to develop a strategy to provide an adequate ministry for the smaller churches in the midst of social change.

One factor not hitherto mentioned which made possible the establishment of new churches was the creation of a new church loan fund. This made it possible for a respectable first unit to be built to house the newly organized church. In recent years bonding programs have also been employed with a considerable degree of success in financing the erection of new churches. In such programs the Board of Finance has provided guidance.

EDUCATIONAL INSTITUTIONS

Following the close of World War II, the enrollment of students in Bethel College increased beyond all previous records. Furthermore, beginning in 1945, Bethel College shared to a much greater degree in the denominational budget than before. The Program of Achievement provided a substantial increase in the permanent endowment funds of the college besides providing a new building to house the library. Serious consideration began to be given shortly before the beginning of the decade to the possibility of the college's achieving full accreditation, and in November, 1953, this goal was realized when Bethel College was admitted to membership in the Southern Association of Colleges and Schools.

Meanwhile, the erection of the Library-Seminary Building helped give an identity to the Cumberland Presbyterian Theological Seminary which it had not enjoyed for many years. Prior to 1951 the enrollment in the Seminary had been small. In the fall quarter of 1951, the Seminary opened its first session in the new building with an enrollment of twenty-six students. By the spring of 1952 the number had increased to thirty-two. Subsequently, a new high of fifty-seven students was reached in the fall of 1955.

In June, 1955, a memorial was addressed to the General Assembly by Memphis Presbytery asking that consideration be given to moving Bethel College and the Cumberland Presbyterian Theological Seminary to Memphis, Tennessee. Upon recommendation of the Committee on Higher Education of the General Assembly, a committee of eleven men was appointed to accept overtures from any city interested in having the college and seminary located within its bounds and to report its findings and recommendations to the 1956 General Assembly. This committee, after much study, reported that the relocation of Bethel College was impractical but recommended that the Cumberland Presbyterian Theological Seminary be separated from Bethel College and relocated in Memphis, Tennessee. The General Assembly in 1956 adopted a recommendation that the theological department be separated from Bethel College and a theological seminary be established to be governed by a Board of Trustees. It also adopted a recommendation that the Seminary be relocated in a metropolitan area following a restudy of the curriculum and when adequate financial resources should be available to provide for an effective theological program.

The new Board of Trustees immediately gave its attention to these matters and, upon assurances from representatives of Memphis that support would be given such a campaign, the Board of Trustees recommended to the General Assembly in 1957 that the Cumberland Presbyterian Theological Seminary be relocated in Memphis upon the condition that an acceptable site and $500,000 be provided by the Memphis community. This recommendation was approved by the General Assembly.

Before the next General Assembly, however, difficulties arose in the matter of setting up an organization for such a campaign, and the financial recession which occurred in the spring of 1958 resulted in the cancellation of plans for the campaign. The General Assembly meeting in Birmingham, Alabama, in June, 1958, reaffirmed the previously expressed intention of relocating the Seminary in an urban area as soon as feasible. No further action relative to relocation was taken during the decade.

CO-OPERATION AND RESISTANCE

One of the most controversial actions taken by the Cumberland Presbyterian Church during the 1950's, and at the same time one which was symbolic of the spiritual unity Cumberland Presbyterians feel with other Christian people, involved the membership of certain agencies of the General Assembly in some of the divisions of the National Council of the Churches of Christ in the United States of America. Since the experiences of the attempted union in 1906, Cumberland Presbyterians had tended to be cautious at the point of involvement in interdenominational organizations; however, the Board of Publication and Christian Education prior to 1950 held membership in the International Council of Religious Education, and the Board of Foreign Missions held membership in the Foreign Missions Conference and the Missionary Education Movement. In 1950, the Board of Missions and Evangelism reported that it had applied for membership in the Home Missions Council of North America and the Missionary Education Movement. At the 1950 General Assembly a question was raised concerning the legality of such affiliations. A General Assembly deliverance of 1945 regarding the question of the General Assembly's power to vote the church into membership in any organization outside the church itself was cited. The question was referred to the General Assembly's Permanent Committee on Judiciary for study.

In 1951, the Permanent Committee on Judiciary submitted a majority and a minority report. The majority report, which was adopted by the General Assembly, was to the effect that such affiliation, when approved by the General Assembly, is legal provided it does not involve either the surrender of the autonomy of the General Assembly, board or agency, or any doctrinal change or commitment. Meanwhile, in December, 1950, the above mentioned interdenominational organizations, along with some others, merged to form the National Council of Churches of Christ in the United States of America, with various program divisions. The General Assembly in 1951 gave permission to the Board of Missions and Evangelism to hold membership in the Joint Commission on Missionary Education of the National Council of Churches, the Home Missions Division of the National Council, and the Protestant Indian Council of Oklahoma.

The General Assembly in 1952 had before it memorials from ten presbyteries and one synod opposing any sort of affiliation with the National Council of Churches. The General Assembly, while directing that already existing connections with the National Council remain unsevered for the time being, appointed a fact finding committee composed of four ministers to assemble documentary facts concerning the National Council.

The report of the committee emphasized that existing affiliations with divisions of the National Council of Churches in no way compromised the autonomy of the Cumberland Presbyterian Church or its agencies. The report was approved by the next General Assembly by a large majority. That opposition continued, however, was evidenced by the fact that memorials had been submitted from ten presbyteries opposing affiliation with the National Council. Five presbyteries had requested that existing connections with divisions of the National Council of Churches be maintained. Following the adjournment of the General Assembly a group of ministers and ruling elders held a meeting in which a "Fellowship of Conservative Cumberland Presbyterians" was formed. Besides opposing affiliation of any of the General Assembly agencies with the National Council of Churches, this group expressed opposition to the use of the Revised Standard Version of the Bible which had recently been published. In November, 1953, the "conservative" group held an "assembly" at Huntsville, Alabama, which elected a moderator and stated clerk and urged the organization of the "conservatives" on a presbyterial level.

The General Assembly in 1954 ruled that this organization had acted illegally in applying the name Cumberland Presbyterian to the group and reaffirmed the right of the boards and agencies of the church to maintain existing memberships in divisions of the National Council. Several ministers and a few churches withdrew from the denomination over this issue, and at least two ministers were deposed from the ministry by their presbyteries because of their activities in connection with the Fellowship of Conservative Cumberland Presbyterians. The question of affiliation of boards and agencies with divisions of the National Council of Churches soon ceased to be a live issue.

In 1956, the General Assembly voted to accept the invitation to become a member of the North American section of the World Presbyterian Alliance in which the Cumberland Presbyterian Church had allowed its membership to lapse following 1906. Thus the spiritual unity of the Cumberland Presbyterian Church with all Christians, and especially with other members of the Presbyterian family, was recognized.

THE MID-CENTURY SPIRITUAL ADVANCE

The General Assembly's Planning Committee, acting in response to a General Assembly directive passed in 1953, proposed to the 1954 General Assembly a "Mid-Century Spiritual

Advance." Emphasis would be given to various themes designed
to build up the spiritual life of the church during the period
leading up to the observance of the one hundred fiftieth anni-
versary, in 1960, of the organization of the Cumberland Presbyterian Church. The themes chosen were as follows:

> 1955—Religion in the Home
> 1956—Tithing
> 1957—Churchmanship
> 1958—Evangelism
> 1959—Missions
> 1960—A Year of Jubilee

These themes were widely employed throughout the Cumberland
Presbyterian Church. Results in the spiritual realm are difficult
to measure; however, it may be pointed out that the number of
tithers from January, 1955, to January, 1957, within which period
the subject of tithing was emphasized, rose from 9,088 to 10,698.
Also, the number of conversions reported in 1958, the year
evangelism was emphasized, was 3,066 as compared with 2,690
the preceding year.

The Mid-Century Spiritual Advance was climaxed by a
financial effort to raise the sum of $600,000 as a Mid-Century
Expansion and Development Fund to be used as follows: Bethel
College, $100,000; the Cumberland Presbyterian Theological
Seminary, $100,000; new church loan fund, $100,000; development of denominational conference ground, $100,000; Children's
Home, $15,000; addition to printing plant, $60,000; and denominational birthplace shrine, $25,000. This campaign was officially
launched at the General Assembly in 1959. By the time of the
meeting of the General Assembly in 1960, individuals and
churches had made pledges and commitments totaling $552,000.

The Year of Jubilee was appropriately observed by the General Assembly meeting in Nashville, Tennessee, in 1960. An out-
standing feature of the observance was the pilgrimage to the
birthplace of the Cumberland Presbyterian Church some forty
miles west of Nashville. An estimated three thousand Cumberland
Presbyterians assembled on the hill overlooking the birthplace of

the Cumberland Presbyterian Church to participate in the singing of "Whosoever Will" and to witness a pageant, "The Miracle of 1800." The chapel at the birthplace, made possible by the Mid-Century Expansion and Development program, was ready for inspection on this occasion, and a member of the Birthplace Shrine Commission presented to the moderator of the General Assembly a symbolic key to the shrine indicating the delivery of the completed shrine to the church as a whole.

SOMETHING TO THINK ABOUT

1. What population changes have taken place in your community since 1940? What do such changes indicate as to the direction the missions program of the church should take?

2. Should an urban church in a changing community follow its people by relocating in a suburban community, or should it remain in its original location and change the focus of its ministry? Give reasons for your answer.

3. What is the purpose of the Ministers' In-Service Training School? What justification is there for spending missions money to finance this type of program?

4. How does the usual procedure in establishing a mission church today differ from that generally followed in the Cumberland Presbyterian Church twenty to forty years ago? What new policies have aided the development of the missions program?

5. Has your presbytery or synod recently attempted the establishment of a new church or churches? If so, have you visited one of its mission churches? How has the promotion of presbyterial or synodic missions projects affected your local church? your presbytery? What is the current status of these projects? If any have failed, what were the causes?

6. What were the main developments in the field of higher education in the Cumberland Presbyterian Church during the decade of the fifties?

7. What is the nature of the relationship of the Cumberland Presbyterian Church to the National Council of Churches of Christ in the United States of America? with the World Presbyterian Alliance?

8. What values came to your local church through the Mid-Century Spiritual Advance?

9. What has been accomplished with the money raised through the Mid-Century Expansion and Development Program?

10. What is the present membership of the new churches established during the fifties? How much did these churches contribute to Our United Outreach last year?

13. Serving in the Sixties

Prior to the "Year of Jubilee" attention was being given to the formulation of a continuing emphasis which would build upon the results of the Mid-Century Spiritual Advance program. The committee appointed to recommend the areas of emphasis chose as a basis for the continuing program the theme "God's Call—Be My Servant," based on Isaiah 49:6:

> "It is too light a thing that you should be my servant
> to raise up the tribes of Jacob
> and to restore the preserved of Israel;
> I will give you as a light to the nations,
> that my salvation may reach to the end of the earth"
> (RSV).

Just as God called Israel, his servant, not merely to restore the remnant of Israel but to be a means through which salvation should be carried to the nations, God calls the church, the new Israel, to be God's servant to proclaim the good news of salvation through Christ to all men. The Cumberland Presbyterian Church shares in this mission, not in isolation, but in co-operation with all other branches of Christ's church. The interpretation of the gospel held by Cumberland Presbyterians, with its emphasis that "Christ died not for a part only, but for all mankind," lends a sense of urgency to the mission which we share and, at the same time, offers the possibilities for the success of the mission.

A TIME OF RENEWAL AND OUTREACH

The central concerns to which the Cumberland Presbyterian Church should address itself, the committee believed, were (1) Spiritual Renewal, (2) Christian Outreach, and (3) Leadership Development. To this end themes of a theological nature have been emphasized in successive years. The theme for 1961-1962 was "Renewal—By the Power of the Spirit." That for 1962-1963 was "Servants—Obedient to God's Word." During 1963-1964 the theme was "By God's Grace: A Covenant People." The theme chosen for 1964-1965 was "By God's Grace: A Kingdom of Priests." Themes tentatively chosen for the ensuing years include: 1965-1966, "Servants—Entrusted wtih the Gospel"; and 1966-1967, "Servants—Walk Worthily of Your Calling."

EXPANSION OF THE HOME MISSIONS PROGRAM

The 1961 annual report of the Board of Missions and Evangelism showed that it had under its supervision twenty-six mission projects in various stages of development. Work had been organized in the Atlanta, Georgia, area under the sponsorship of the board of missions of Chattanooga Presbytery. A missionary pastor had been placed at Trona, California, to work with a group of people who desired to become a Cumberland Presbyterian church. Plans were in the making to have a student minister work during the summer with a group at Batesville, Arkansas. A new church had been organized during 1960 at Kosciusko, Mississippi.

By the spring of 1962, there were thirty-six projects under the supervision of the General Assembly's Board. New churches had been organized during 1961 at Trona, California; Frayser (Memphis); Tullahoma, Tennessee; and Faith Church, San Antonio, Texas.

In the spring of 1963, there were thirty-three urban missions and three parishes under the supervision of the General Assembly's Board, and thirteen other projects had received counsel and support from some presbyterial or synodic board. Churches organized during 1962 included Bethany, Louisville, Kentucky; Mayfield, Kentucky; and Whitehaven, Memphis, Tennessee.

At least six churches are known to have been organized during 1963: Faith Church, Batesville, Arkansas; Leitchfield and Harrodsburg, Kentucky; New Providence, Clarksville, Tennessee; Parkwood, Nashville, Tennessee; and a congregation in Chicago. During 1964 churches were organized at Salem and Morrilton, Arkansas, and a new church at Austin, Texas, known as St. Paul's, was organized. The following fellowships were in existence at this writing: University Heights, Tampa, Florida, where the first unit of a church building is under construction; St. Luke's, Fort Worth, Texas; Cromwell, Memphis, Tennessee; Independence, Missouri, and Fayetteville, Arkansas. The work at Fayetteville involves the relocation and revival of a church which had become inactive.

RELOCATION OF THE THEOLOGICAL SEMINARY

The question of relocating the Cumberland Presbyterian Theological Seminary was revived early in 1961 when a conference of interested persons was called to meet at Nashville to consider the possibilities of locating the Seminary in the vicinity of Vanderbilt University in Nashville. Subsequently, Tennessee Synod in a called meeting memorialized the General Assembly asking for an early decision to locate the seminary in Nashville. The General Assembly, which met that year in Florence, Alabama, adopted a recommendation "that the Board of Trustees give consideration to McKenzie and to every possible urban area and make a selection for the location of the Seminary and present the same to the 132nd General Assembly." The board was also directed to present the needs of the seminary in the light of requirements for accreditation by the American Association of Theological Schools and to work out, in conjunction with the Board of Finance, a financial program for meeting these needs.

The Board of Trustees at its spring meeting in 1962 considered proposals submitted by representatives of Nashville, Memphis, and McKenzie. Memphis was recommended to the General Assembly as the location. A site at the southeast corner of East Parkway and Union Extended was selected from among those considered. Memphis Presbytery, working through a commission, secured an option on the site until after the meeting of the General Assembly. Thus the church, again true to its heritage, moved in the direction of establishing its theological school in an area where there was a need for such an institution. Memphis had no theological seminary.

Meanwhile, there had been submitted to the General Assembly in 1961, through the report of the Board of Missions and Evangelism, a recommendation that a priority study be made. It was recognized that the church had many needs and that not all of them could be met immediately. It was suggested that these needs be put in the order of their priority according to the best judgment of the church. Consequently, each board and agency was requested to submit its program and needs for the next several years to the Planning Committee at its fall meeting. This was done, and the priority study was begun. At the spring meeting, 1962, the Planning Committee recommended that the Seminary be given priority insofar as a financial campaign was concerned. Toward the end of the decade a financial campaign for missions was to be promoted. Development of a denominational conference ground as proposed by the Board of Publication and Christian Education was postponed indefinitely.

The General Assembly, which met in Little Rock, Arkansas, in June, 1962, adopted the recommendation that the seminary be given priority. It approved the recommendation that the seminary be relocated in Memphis and appointed a commission composed of three laymen in Memphis to purchase suitable property and put it in order for the use of the seminary. Provision was also made for a committee of three to visit the seminary and make an evaluation of its whole program.

Following the Assembly, the Board of Finance purchased the property at East Parkway and Union Extended for the seminary. The purchase price was $95,000. During the ensuing year, plans for a financial campaign to be known as the Seminary Development Program were formulated for presentation to the 1963 General Assembly. The plans as submitted to the Assembly called for the raising of $450,000 for the Seminary from the following sources: Memphis Presbytery and the Memphis area, $125,000; individual gifts outside of Memphis, $125,000; and churches outside of Memphis Presbytery, $200,000. The money thus raised was to be used as follows: $100,000 to cover cost of property held for the seminary by the Board of Finance; $40,000 for renovation of the existing building located on the property; $60,000 for erection of a library building; $40,000 to be used as a down payment on student housing; and $210,000 for permanent endowment. Memphis Presbytery in the fall of 1963 assigned shares totaling $25,000 to its churches. The remaining $100,000 requested of the Memphis area was to be solicited from individuals and corporations in the Memphis area.

The Board of Trustees in its meeting in the summer of 1963 voted to begin operation of the seminary in its new location in September, 1964. In February, 1964, contracts were let for the renovation of the existing building and erection of the library building. The timetable thus adopted gave a sense of urgency to the campaign. Discussion of a possible relocation of the Seminary had been going on since 1955. Now the time for action had come. In September, 1964, the seminary opened its doors for the new school year in Memphis. By action of the 1964 General Assembly, the seminary had a new name—Memphis Theological Seminary of the Cumberland Presbyterian Church.

THE COVENANT LIFE CURRICULUM [1]

For many years, the only church school curriculum materials available through official church channels were based on the Uniform Series. Over the years, changes were made in the curriculum plan for children, and later for youth, so that the Cycle Graded Series came into use. The church produced a number of curriculum pieces for adults and young people, but because of high production costs and low circulation possibilities it was not able to produce all the materials needed in children's classes. Supplementary materials from a variety of sources were recommended to local churches and were distributed by the Board of Publication and Christian Education.

Prior to and especially during the 1950's, movements began in most of the Protestant denominations to make major changes in the curriculum materials being produced and recommended. In some instances, denominations joined with others of similar theological position to seek an improved plan for curriculum for their several constituencies. The Board of Publication and Christian Education, because of limited staff time and budget, was unable to participate actively in any such undertaking. However, staff members kept in touch with current developments in the various denominations.

In 1962, after much study and evaluation, the Board of Publication and Christian Education recommended that the General Assembly adopt the Covenant Life Curriculum as the official curriculum of the Cumberland Presbyterian Church. This curriculum plan had been under development since 1955 by the Presbyterian Church in the United States, the Reformed Church in America, the Moravian Church in America, and the United Presbyterian Church of North America (which merged in 1958 with the Presbyterian Church in the United States of America). Throughout the development of this curriculum, members of the Board's staff had been invited to participate in the development of the curriculum, and had done so as they were able. The 1962 General Assembly approved the recommendation of the Board. Since that time, the Associate Reformed Presbyterian Church has also approved the use of the Covenant Life Curriculum, and some other denominations have use of the curriculum under study as this is written.

The Covenant Life Curriculum plan embraces the total life of the church and has a potential for much good beyond the church school as it is usually understood. The wide scope of the curriculum may be seen in its three aspects or settings where learning takes place: systematic study (church school), home and family nurture, and worship and work of the congregation. The depth of the curriculum plan is evident in the three approaches to systematic study—the Bible, the church, the Christian life—which constitute the three major alternating themes for church school study. (The course you are studying is part of the second or church approach.)

Adults began study of the Covenant Life Curriculum in church school (systematic study) in 1963, and youth began study in 1964. As this is written, materials are being printed for use in children's classes beginning in the fall of 1965. A few congregations have started a serious attempt to make use of the ideas and materials offered in the home and family nurture aspect. Even though many local churches have not yet undertaken study of the Covenant Life Curriculum (Uniform Series lessons are still available for adults and youth), this plan does put the major responsibility for curriculum where it must be—in the local church. Insofar as study is taken seriously, this curriculum plan promises local churches new life through the Holy Spirit.

PROPOSED REALIGNMENT OF THE MISSIONS PROGRAM

In its annual report to the General Assembly in 1960, the Board of Foreign Missions expressed the opinion that the time had come for a thorough restudy of the foreign missions program and a consideration of the possibility of a realignment of this program. A committee on realignment, which had been named by the board, continued its study throughout the year and recommended a proposed realignment plan to the 1961 General Assembly. Since 1906 the Board of Foreign Missions (earlier known as the Woman's Board of Missions) had exercised exclusive oversight of the foreign missions work of the church. The foreign missions work had been financed largely through the woman's missionary auxiliaries, although special days provided an opportunity for church-wide participation in this work.

The plan as proposed to the General Assembly in 1961 was intended to accomplish two purposes: First, it would involve the whole church in the work of foreign missions, and second, it would involve the women of the church in the total work of the church. Specifically, it was proposed that the work of foreign missions would be supervised by a Board of Foreign Missions to consist of six men and three women. There would also be a Board of Women's Work composed of nine women. Three of these would also serve on the Board of Foreign Missions. The Missionary Convention held annually at the same time and place as the General Assembly would become the Convention of the Women of the Church. Their program of work would include not only information and inspiration with reference to foreign missions but would deal with other phases of the denominational program as well. The General Assembly in 1961 authorized the board to continue its study and to present a more detailed report to the 1962 Assembly. Meanwhile local church manuals for the world missions program and for Cumberland Presbyterian women were prepared.

The General Assembly in 1962 created a Committee on Alignment to plan and correlate the total work of the church. This committee was to consist of one member and an executive of each board of the General Assembly with the stated clerk of the Assembly serving as chairman. It was felt by some that more was involved than just the work of foreign missions. The new committee recommended that there be one missions manual for the local church which would include both the work of world missions and that of missions and evangelism. It was recommended that there be one missions committee in the local church to be responsible for the emphasis of world missions, home missions, and evangelism. It was recommended that January 1, 1965, be the date for the initiation of this program. The recommendations of the Board of Foreign Missions relative to the two boards, namely, the Board of World Missions and the Board of Women's Work, remained substantially as originally proposed. Six of the seven recommendations of the committee were approved by the General Assembly, and it was decided that the effective date of realignment should be January 1, 1965.

The General Assembly which met at Chattanooga, Tennessee, in June, 1964, reconsidered the plan of alignment and adopted a proposal that there be one Board of Missions. This Board is composed of fifteen members with the provision that at any time there must be at least six men and at least six women on the Board. This Board is to assume the responsibility for the missions program of the church following the 1965 General Assembly. In creating this Board the General Assembly took action changing its standing rule on board membership so as to provide that members of boards and legal agencies may be "ordained ministers, ordained elders, or members of the Cumberland Presbyterian Church, either men or women, in good standing, and active in the local church in which membership is held."

SOME RECENT TRENDS

During the past ten years, the Cumberland Presbyterian Church has demonstrated in various ways its willingness to co-operate with Christians of other denominations. In 1956, the Cumberland Presbyterian Church became a member of the North American Section of the World Presbyterian Alliance. More recently, in 1961, an amendment to the Constitution was adopted making it possible for a Cumberland Presbyterian minister serving a parish composed in part of a church or churches of another denomination to become an associate member of the other denomination without disturbing his status as a Cumberland Presbyterian minister. In like manner, the amendment provided for a minister of another church who has been called to serve in a parish of which one or more Cumberland Presbyterian churches are constituents to hold associate membership in the presbytery of the Cumberland Presbyterian Church in which such church or churches are situated. In 1962 a Committee on Inter-Church Relations was created. At the General Assembly at Little Rock in 1962, the Assembly was made to rejoice and to feel humble when Dr. W. Glen Harris, of Birmingham, Michigan, spoke as the fraternal delegate from the United Presbyterian Church, U. S. A. His message delivered by request of his General Assembly contained an apology for wrongs done by that church toward the Cumberland Presbyterian Church, both during the years shortly before and after 1810 and during the period just following 1906. The General Assembly accepted the apology and at the same time asked the forgiveness of the United Presbyterian Church, U. S. A. "for any unchristian attitude that our communion, the Cumberland Presbyterian Church, may have displayed toward them in the past."

In several instances there has been a realignment of presbyteries resulting in a smaller number of presbyteries. In 1961 the Synod of Oklahoma reduced the number of its presbyteries from four to three. In 1962 the Synod of Tennessee reduced the number of its presbyteries from six to three. The Synod of Missouri has approved reorganization of two presbyteries as one new presbytery effective in July 1965. In 1960, on the other hand, the Synod of Arkansas disapproved a proposal for the realignment of its presbyteries by a presbyterial vote of five to one. Some judicatories have changed names while maintaining essentially the same boundaries. For example, in 1964, Illinois Synod became North Central Synod.

Presbyterial names and boundaries should never be considered sacrosanct. Many changes in presbyterial and synodical boundaries have been made in nearly every area occupied by the Cumberland Presbyterian Church at various times during its more than one hundred fifty years of history. Others doubtless will yet be made. A question may be raised, however, as to whether it may not be possible for a presbytery to be too large, as well as too small, to function effectively. The presbytery should be aware of the needs of its individual churches as well as have a vital concern for the spiritual welfare of each of them. It may be suggested, too, that there is value in maintaining a situation in which every member of presbytery may feel free to participate fully in the decisions of the presbytery.

THE GENIUS OF THE CUMBERLAND
PRESBYTERIAN CHURCH

The Cumberland Presbyterian Church had its origin on the frontier as the direct result of an effort of certain ministers to follow the direction of the Holy Spirit to meet the needs of the frontier. Its founders proved themselves capable of making the necessary adaptations in revival methods, in the matter of ministerial education, and in permitting exceptions to be made in the acceptance of the Confession of Faith of the Presbyterian Church by those who were licensed or ordained. Within four years after the organization of the first presbytery of the new church, they took the further liberty of revising the Confession of Faith so that it would conform more nearly to their understanding of the gospel of Christ. Some sixty years later their grandsons again revised the Confession of Faith to bring it more nearly into conformity with what was generally believed and preached by Cumberland Presbyterians.

In recent years the Cumberland Presbyterian Church has again manifested that adaptability to changing circumstances which characterized its founders. It approved a rather thorough reorganization of denominational boards and agencies in 1948. It has adopted the Covenant Life Curriculum, a new plan for Christian education. It has seen the necessity of taking the church to people where they are, and has established churches in the centers of population while at the same time attempting to care for the spiritual needs of those people who remain in the rural areas.

In 1927 and 1929, amendments were proposed and subsequently adopted which made it more difficult than formerly to amend the Confession of Faith and Constitution. These amendments were adopted for the avowed purpose of safeguarding the interests of the church and preventing a recurrence of what happened in 1904-1905 when a minority of votes within the presbyteries were so distributed as to carry a majority of presbyteries for the proposed union with the Presbyterian Church, U. S. A. The passage of these amendments was criticized by some who asserted that it would never be possible to make any further changes in the Confession of Faith or Constitution. Since 1953, however, no less than six amendments, two to the Confession of Faith and four to the Constitution, have been passed. This indicates that, if the church as a whole really desires a change in its constitutional law, such change can be made, even though an affirmative vote of three-fourths of the presbyteries is now required.

We are now living in a period of great social change. This will doubtless call for further adaptations in program to meet the needs of the new frontiers which must be faced. The Cumberland Presbyterian Church will be true to its heritage, not necessarily by imitating the methods used by its founders, although it may learn something from them, but by adapting its machinery and its methods to serve the present age.

Another feature which has characterized the Cumberland Presbyterian Church has been a wholesome respect for the religious experiences of one's fellow Christians even though one may not agree with them on every detail of faith and practice. The founders of the Cumberland Presbyterian Church early adopted the practice of open communion in contrast to the practice of "fencing" the Lord's table, which prevailed at that time in the Presbyterian Church. Thus they demonstrated the fact that they accepted the personal religious experience of Christians of other denominations.

The revisers of the Confession of Faith in the 1880's consciously avoided including in the revised Confession tenets peculiar to any one man or faction. Although they endeavored to draw with precision the boundary between the Cumberland Presbyterian system of doctrine and other systems, they proposed to grant liberty of opinion within those bounds.

The Confession of Faith does not bind Cumberland Presbyterians to any one theory of the inspiration of Scripture, although it asserts the fact of inspiration. It does not commit those who adhere to its doctrines to any one theory of the atonement. It does not speak dogmatically as to when or how the kingdom of God comes. Within an evangelical framework it grants considerable liberty in matters of detail recognizing that those who differ from one another in their understanding of Scripture may have good grounds for doing so.

Cumberland Presbyterians, to be sure, have held tenaciously to certain convictions regarding the plan of salvation, especially with regard to the provision that God has made for the salvation of all men and the manifestation of the Holy Spirit "with the same intent to every man" to convince men of their need of Christ. Sometimes at great cost these convictions, or the right to hold and preach them, have been maintained. Yet the Cumberland Presbyterian Church has never claimed to have a monopoly on the truth. It recognizes that the Lord has "other sheep, that are not of this fold."

SOMETHING TO THINK ABOUT

1. What could be accomplished through the Cumberland Presbyterian Church if it should indeed be God's servant to proclaim the good news of salvation to the ends of the earth?

2. What values have come from the supervision of mission projects (including those promoted by synods and presbyteries) by the General Assembly's Board of Missions and Evangelism?

3. What enlarged opportunities for service are envisioned for the theological seminary in its new location at Memphis?

4. What values have come to your local church through the use of the Covenant Life Curriculum? How do you understand study of this book as a part of the Covenant Life Curriculum?

5. What was the significance of the message brought by Dr. W. Glen Harris to the General Assembly in 1962 and the General Assembly's response to this message?

6. What are the advantages and disadvantages of large presbyteries as compared with the effectiveness and ineffectiveness of the somewhat smaller presbyteries which still make up a considerable portion of the Cumberland Presbyterian Church?

7. What do you consider the most valuable contributions made by the Cumberland Presbyterian Church during the more than one hundred fifty years of its history?

8. What has been the attitude of the Cumberland Presbyterian Church toward other Christian bodies?

9. What do you envision as the future of the Cumberland Presbyterian Church? of your local congregation?

Notes

CHAPTER 1

1 George P. Fisher, *The Reformation,* new and revised edition (New York: Charles Scribner's Sons, 1926), p. 461.

2 William Warren Sweet, *Our American Churches,* (Nashville: Abingdon-Cokesbury Press, 1924), p. 119.

3 Fisher, *op. cit.,* pp. 460-461.

4 Stanley I. Stuber, *How We Got Our Denominations,* (New York: Association Press, 1959), p. 217.

CHAPTER 2

1 James Arminius, "Declaration of Sentiments," *The Writings of James Arminius,* trans. by James Nichols and W. R. Bagnell (Grand Rapids, Mich.: Baker Book House, 1956), Vol. I, p. 229.

2 *Ibid.,* pp. 237-238.

3 *Ibid.,* p. 247.

4 James Arminius, "Apology," *The Writings of James Arminius,* trans. by James Nichols and W. R. Bagnell, Vol. I, pp. 365-366. See also "Declaration of Sentiments," pp. 252-254.

5 Charles Wesley Lowry, Jr., "Spiritual Antecedents of Anglican Evangelicalism," *Anglican Evangelicalism,* edited by Alexander C. Zabriskie (Philadelphia: The Church Historical Society, 1943), p. 75.

6 *The Journal of the Reverend John Wesley, A. M.* (New York: J. Emory and B. Waugh, 1832), Vol. I, p. 18.

7 *Ibid.,* p. 74.

8 A resolution passed by the Goose Creek Methodist Conference was included in a letter written by L. Blackman, a presiding elder of the Methodist Church, to Cumberland Presbytery under date of March 10, 1811. The resolution was as follows: "*Resolved,* That those who call themselves members of the Cumberland Presbytery are in such a state of accountability to each other, as will authorize us to admit individuals of that body, on examination, to the Lord's Supper with us. An examination we deem necessary to know whether they are regular members, etc."

9 Robert Donnell, *Thoughts on Various Subjects* (Louisville, Ky.: published for the Board of Publication by Rev. Lee Roy Woods, Publishing Agent, 1854), p. 189.

10 William Warren Sweet, *The Story of Religion in America,* revised edition (New York: Harper and Brothers, 1950), pp. 239-240. Otterbein was a minister of the Reformed Church, Boehm a Mennonite. They united with several others in founding the "United Brethren in Christ."

CHAPTER 3

1 William Warren Sweet, *Religion in the Development of American Culture,* (New York: Charles Scribner's Sons, 1952), p. 146.

2 So called to distinguish it from the Great Awakening which began in 1734 under the preaching of Jonathan Edwards.

3 F. R. Cossitt, *Life and Times of Rev. Finis Ewing* (Louisville: Board of Publication of Cumberland Presbyterian Church, 1853), p. 14.

4 Quoted by Sweet, *The Story of Religion in America,* pp. 223-224.

5 Sweet, *Religion in the Development of American Culture,* p. 93.

6 T. C. Anderson, *Life of Rev. George Donnell* (Nashville: Southern Methodist Publishing House, 1858), pp. 88-89.

7 Cossitt, *op. cit.,* p. 97.

8 *Ibid.,* p. 35.

9 *Ibid.,* p. 37.

10 E. B. Crisman, *Origin and Doctrines of the Cumberland Presbyterian Church,* second edition (St. Louis: A. F. Cox, 1858), pp. 21-22.

11 Sweet, *op. cit.,* p. 147.

12 In the account of the revival, McGready's "Narrative of the Commencement and Progress of the Revival of 1800" contained in a letter to a friend dated "Logan County, Kentucky, October 23, 1801" is the source followed except where otherwise noted. From *Posthumous Works of the Reverend and Pious James McGready,* edited by the Reverend James Smith (Louisville: W. W. Worsley, 1831).

13 James Smith, *History of the Cumberland Presbyterian Church* (Nashville: Cumberland Presbyterian Office, 1835), pp. 565-566. Smith quotes the entire covenant.

14 Sweet, *op. cit.,* p. 148.

15 Smith, *op. cit.,* p. 563.

16 Anderson, *op. cit.,* pp. 56-57.

17 McGready's "Narrative."

18 Smith, *op. cit.,* p. 589.

19 Copied from *The Revivalist,* January 9, 1833, in *The Theological Medium,* July, 1876, pp. 262-263.

20 *Ibid.,* p. 269.

CHAPTER 4

1 Constitution of the Presbyterian Church in the United States of America, "Form of Government," Chap. XIV, sec. VI.

2 An intermediate session of presbytery was one appointed to be held between the regular meetings to transact some particular business such as

the ordination of a minister. The presbytery in its regular meeting would specify who should attend and what business was to be transacted. Such an intermediate session functioned very much like a presbyterial commission functions today.

3 According to the minutes of the commission, the reason for the request was "that they might confer together." According to statements of members of the revival party who were present, the request was for time that they might pray.

4 Robert Davidson, *History of the Presbyterian Church in the State of Kentucky,* (New York: Robert Carter, 1847), p. 250.

5 *Ibid.,* pp. 255-256.

6 Cossitt, *Life and Times of Rev. Finis Ewing,* pp. 168-169.

CHAPTER 5

1 B. W. McDonnold, *History of the Cumberland Presbyterian Church,* (Nashville: Board of Publication of the Cumberland Presbyterian Church, 1888), p. 112.

2 Journal of W. A. Scott made available through the courtesy of Dr. C. M. Drury, of San Francisco Theological Seminary.

3 These figures do not include urban missions sponsored by presbyteries and synods and not under direction of the General Assembly's Board.

CHAPTER 6

1 McDonnold, *History of the Cumberland Presbyterian Church,* p. 411.

2 Cossitt, *Life and Times of Rev. Finis Ewing,* p. 275, n.

3 Minutes of General Assembly, 1848, pp. 12-13.

4 Minutes of Hopewell Presbytery, September 7, 1848.

5 For this observation I am indebted to a seminar paper by the Rev. William Rustenhaven entitled "Attitudes Toward Slavery Within the Cumberland Presbyterian Church," which he prepared for a history class in State University of Iowa, 1963.

6 McDonnold, *op. cit.,* p. 418.

7 *Ibid.,* chapter XL.

8 One is the Cumberland Presbyterian Church at Charlotte, Tennessee. Another is at Ro Ellen, near Dyersburg, Tennessee. Actually the latter building was erected in 1866 but it is understood that the balcony was for the Negro worshipers according to the established practice.

9 Session records of Corsicana (Texas) Cumberland Presbyterian Church, 1853-1870, p. 53.

10 Minutes of Texas Presbytery, September 14, 1838.

11 Minutes of General Assembly, 1866, pp. 80-81.

12 Minutes of Hopewell Presbytery, fall meeting, 1867.

13 Minutes of Hopewell Presbytery, spring meeting, 1868.

14 Minutes of New Hope Presbytery, July, 1866.

15 Minutes of New Hope Presbytery, December 7, 1867.

16 Sweet, *The Story of Religion in America,* p. 329.

17 Minutes of General Assembly, 1869, pp. 23-24.

18 Minutes of General Assembly, 1871, p. 28.

19 McDonnold, *op. cit.,* p. 436.

20 Minutes of General Assembly, 1873, p. 31.

21 Hope Church, Chicago, was a constituent of Chicago Presbytery.

22 *The Cumberland Presbyterian,* January 14, 1926.

23 In about 1958 the General Assembly of the Cumberland Presbyterian Church, Colored, voted to drop the word "Colored" from its name. Later it adopted the name "The Cumberland Presbyterian Church in the United States and Liberia." In 1960 it voted to call itself the "Second Cumberland Presbyterian Church." Within recent years the Colored Methodist Episcopal Church has changed its name to "Christian Methodist Episcopal."

CHAPTER 7

1 Thomas Forester, "In Memory of Those Who Went Before Us," *The Missionary Messenger,* Vol. 31, No. 3 (March, 1960), pp. 16ff.

CHAPTER 8

1 Richard Beard, *Brief Biographical Sketches of Some of the Early Ministers of the Cumberland Presbyterian Church* (Nashville: Southern Methodist Publishing House, 1867), p. 38.

2 F. R. Cossitt, *Life and Times of Rev. Finis Ewing,* pp. 281, 288-289, 490-494.

3 J. B. Logan, *History of the Cumberland Presbyterian Church in Illinois* (Alton, Illinois: Perrin and Smith, 1878), p. 122.

4 McDonnold, *History of the Cumberland Presbyterian Church,* p. 60.

5 Richard Beard, "Brief Historical Sketch of Cumberland College, at Princeton, Kentucky, 1825-1861," *Theological Medium,* 1876, p. 141.

6 Alfred Charles True, *A History of Agricultural Education in the United States* (Washington, 1929), pp. 33 ff.

7 McDonnold, *op. cit.,* p. 525.

8 Winstead Paine Bone, *A History of Cumberland University* (published by the Author, Lebanon, Tennessee, 1935), p. 275.

9 McDonnold, *op. cit.,* p. 557.

10 At least one other school was being operated in Missouri under Cumberland Presbyterian auspices during this time, namely, Ozark College, at Greenfield, which belonged to Ozark Presbytery.

11 H. B. Evans, "History of the Organization and Administration of Cumberland Presbyterian Colleges," unpublished doctoral dissertation, George Peabody College for Teachers, pp. 306-309.

CHAPTER 9

1 McDonnold, *History of the Cumberland Presbyterian Church,* p. 603. In 1829, "The Form of Government" had been revised to provide for a General Assembly.

2 Report of Committees appointed by the General Assembly to revise the Confession of Faith to the 1882 General Assembly, p. 4.

3 Confession of Faith of the Presbyterian Church, U. S. A., Chapter XX, Section 1.

4 Confession of Faith of the Cumberland Presbyterian Church, section 71.

5 In 1903 the Presbyterian Church, U. S. A., amended its Confession of Faith by adding chapters on "the Holy Spirit" and "the Love of God and Missions." It also added a "Declaratory Statement" intended to interpret Chapter III and Chapter X, Section 3. (For the full text of the "Declaratory Statement" see page 126.) More recently the Presbyterian Church, U. S., inserted in its Confession of Faith a chapter on "the Holy Spirit" almost identical with that adopted by the Presbyterian Church, U. S. A., in 1903, and a chapter on "the Gospel" which is identical with the chapter on "the Love of God and Missions" adopted by its sister church in 1903. In both instances, however, the text of the chapters which were most unacceptable to Cumberland Presbyterians was left unaltered.

CHAPTER 10

1 The Constitution of the Presbyterian Church in the United States of America (Philadelphia: Presbyterian Board of Publication and Sabbath-School Work, 1903), p. 138b.

2 Minutes of General Assembly, Presbyterian Church, U. S. A., 1904, p. 129.

3 Minutes of General Assembly, Cumberland Presbyterian Church, 1906, p. 79.

CHAPTER 13

1 By agreement between the writer and the staff of the Board of Publication and Christian Education, the section on the Covenant Life Curriculum was written by the Board staff.

THOMAS HARDESTY CAMPBELL, who is Dean of Memphis Theological Seminary, was born near Santa Anna, Texas. He attended Daniel Baker College at Brownwood, Texas, and in 1927 received the A.B. degree from Bethel College. In 1929, he received the B.D. degree from the Cumberland Presbyterian Theological Seminary. Southern Methodist University awarded him the M.A. degree in 1938, and he has done additional graduate study at the University of Chicago. In 1949, Bethel College conferred on him the honorary D.D. degree.

During Dr. Campbell's early ministry, he was pastor of small town and country churches in Texas and Louisiana. He assisted in organizing the Cumberland Presbyterian Church in Shreveport, Louisiana (now Highland Avenue Church), and served as its pastor from 1939-1942. In addition to pastoral responsibilities, he served as editor of *The Cumberland Crusader* from 1935-1944. Beginning as a teacher in 1944, he has served in several capacities in the educational institutions of the church. He has been Dean and Acting Administrator of Bethel College, and has served as Dean and President of the Cumberland Presbyterian Theological Seminary.

Dr. Campbell was married to Nellie McClellan of Lubbock, Texas, and they were the parents of one daughter, Jo Nell, now Mrs. J. S. Reynolds, of Odessa, Missouri. Following the death of Mrs. Campbell, he married Margaret Estes, a native of Oklahoma, and they have three grown sons, Samuel Henry, Thomas Dishman, and Paul David. The family also includes five grandsons.

Dr. Campbell has written two previous books dealing with the history of the denomination. They are *A History of the Cumberland Presbyterian Church in Texas* and *Studies in Cumberland Presbyterian History*. He is also the author of *A Crown of Glorying* (dealing with I Thessalonians) and *The Ministering Church,* both study booklets prepared for use within the denomination.